Spirituality and Couples:
Heart and Soul
in the Therapy Process

Spirituality
and Couples:
Heart and Soul
in the Therapy Process

Barbara Jo Brothers
Editor

Routledge
Taylor & Francis Group

NEW YORK AND LONDON

First published 1992 by Haworth Press, Inc

This edition published 2016 by Routledge
711 Third Avenue, New York, NY 10017, USA
2 Park Square, Milton Park, Abingdon, Oxfordshire OX14 4RN

First issued in paperback 2016

Routledge is an imprint of the Taylor & Francis Group, an informa business

Spirituality and Couples: Heart and Soul in the Therapy Process has also been published as
Journal of Couples Therapy, Volume 3, Number 1 1992.

Library of Congress Cataloging-in-Publication Data

Spirituality and couples : heart and soul in the therapy process / Barbara Jo Brothers, editor.
     p. cm.
     "Has also been published as Journal of couples therapy, volume 3, number 1 1992"-T.p.
verso.
     Includes bibliographical references.
     ISBN 1-56024-312-0 (alk. paper)
     1. Marital psychotherapy. 2. Spirituality. I. Brothers, Barbara, 1940- .
RC488.5.S7 1993
616.89'156-dc20
                                             93-4262
                                               CIP

ISBN 13: 978-1-138-98279-6 (pbk)
ISBN 13: 978-1-56024-312-0 (hbk)

Spirituality and Couples: Heart and Soul in the Therapy Process

Spirituality and Couples: Heart and Soul in the Therapy Process

CONTENTS

ABOUT THE EDITOR

Barbara Jo Brothers, MSW, BCD, a Diplomate in Clinical Social Work, National Association of Social Workers, is in private practice in New Orleans. She received her BA from the University of Texas and her MSW from Tulane University, where she is currently on the faculty. She was editor of *The Newsletter of the American Academy of Psychotherapists* from 1976 to 1985, and was Associate Editor of *Voices: The Art and Science of Psychotherapy* from 1979 to 1989. She has nearly 30 years of experience, in both the public and private sectors, helping people to form skills that will enable them to connect emotionally. The author of numerous articles and book chapters on authenticity in human relating, she has advocated healthy, congruent communication that builds intimacy as opposed to destructive, incongruent communication which blocks intimacy. In addition to her many years of direct work with couples and families, Ms. Brothers had led numerous workshops on teaching communication in families and has also played an integral role in the development of training programs in family therapy for mental health workers throughout the Louisiana state mental health system. She is a board member of the Institute for International Connections, a non-profit organization for cross-cultural professional development, focused on training and cross-cultural exchange with psychotherapists in Russia, republics once part of what used to be the Soviet Union, and other Eastern European countries.

Preface

Why an issue on spirituality in a journal on couples therapy?

Because most of us agree there exists in us an indefinable life force. Given this factor's existence, it would be a mistake to ignore that existence if we accept systems theory as viable. Definable and "locate-able" or not, spirit or life force is part of the mind/body/spirit system that constitutes a human being.

Stepping somewhat beyond the point at which "we mostly all agree," I would like to suggest that there also exists a higher self, or, at least, the possibility of a higher self, in therapists and patients alike. That possibility being presumed, it would seem reasonable to explore the nature of the meeting of higher selves in the course of relationship. In fact, it would seem important to do so.

Given that I was writing this introduction on the eve of election day in Louisiana as David Duke, former head of the Ku Klux Klan, was running for governor, I was probably more aware than usual of the importance of *recognition of manipulation*. It is no trick for therapists to make an assessment of David Duke's personality structure. What concerns me is that there is far less concern, among therapists as well as the general public, about the toxic potential in the phenomenon of human beings treating each other as objects. Treating persons as objects to be manipulated is an entree into an insidious process, the inherent structure of which allows the one to have power over the other. Duke is only at the far end of that continuum; he did not invent it.

So I submit this issue as an attempt to focus on "heart and soul" in human relationships in the hope of heading for another continuum entirely. Persons who are experiencing the "high self" potential in themselves operate from a place

xiii

of respecting self and other, not using the other as an object on which to display one's power. I am, of course, presuming a connection between "high self" and the spirit. Since I am in the company of the history of humankind in the presumption, we will also let that connection stand as a given (as this is a psychotherapy volume, not a theological volume).

Be all of that as it may, I believe our pursuit of the manifestation of our high self in our business with each other holds far more promise for high functioning than does learning effective ways to manipulate each other—whether we call it "therapeutic techniques" or winning an election.

Barbara Jo Brothers
Editor

Heart and Soul and Communication: An Interview with Virginia Satir—

Sheldon Starr

[Early in 1985 I asked Virginia Satir if she was willing to be interviewed on videotape concerning her thinking about family therapy at that time and especially with regard to any ideas she might wish to share with the family therapy community. The interview took place on March 15, 1985 at Virginia's home in Menlo Park, California. The transcript of the interview is 60 pages, and this is the *third* of a series of segments from that interview covering different themes. This segment touches on values, ethics, the use of "heart and soul," and manipulation in therapy.]

[The use of brackets [ ] and *underlining* below are editorial additions for the purpose of clarity and/or emphasis.] S.S.

A highly condensed and edited summary of the entire interview appeared in the AFTA Newsletter, Fall 1985 and that version consisted of less than 20% of the interview.

Sheldon Starr, PhD was founder and director for 15 years of the Family Study Unit, a family therapy training and treatment program at the V.A. Medical Center, Palo Alto, CA when this interview was conducted. Dr. Starr is presently Professor of Psychology (part time) at Pacific Graduate School of Psychology and is in private practice, both in Palo Alto, California. His association with Virginia Satir spanned 25 years, first as student, then as associate and long-time friend. Correspondence may be sent to 801 Welch Road, #209, Palo Alto, CA 94304.

1

STARR: I remember you conducted a Family Reconstruction in Santa Cruz and Rich Bandler and John Grinder were watching you work and talking to you, and they were in the midst of developing what's since been called Neuro-Linguistic Programming (NLP). I think it would be interesting to see how you think NLP fits in with *your* concept of Family Therapy.

SATIR: Okay, let me answer on different levels. I have always believed that there is more to whatever I'm seeing than what is there, what I've seen. When Richard and John came along, it was exciting. It would be like somebody had been playing around with light and colors and somebody came along and said "Oh this is what you're doing" and was able to give a name to it and take off that piece and show how that was done. It was marvelous and I enjoyed it at the beginning. When we think of it in terms of family, and watching where and how people physically respond, where they put their eyes, and listening to the different verbs, (one will make a visual verb and somebody else will make an audio verb), well, that's fine to know. Alright, it adds to our understanding about how people put out their learnings without them knowing it. So that was very useful. With people who use this with heart and soul, they have some more techniques at their command. Without it, it's dynamite.

STARR: Without which?

SATIR: Without heart and soul.

STARR: But I'm not following. NLP is dynamite without heart and soul?

SATIR: Right.

STARR: I'm not understanding that one.

SATIR: Now, let us take a very simple thing. Where you look when I ask you a question tells the practitioner where you are in your mind.

STARR: Um huh.

SATIR: Generally speaking, whether you're looking up or down or where, puts a lot of control in the hands of the practitioner, doesn't it?

STARR: Um huh.

SATIR: Then if you don't use heart and soul and ethics with it this can be a terrible thing. That's what I'm saying.

STARR: Yeah, okay. Now I've got you.

SATIR: And there's a lot of that going on. However, thank goodness it's beginning to diminish. But you see when somebody needs to have some way of control, that [if I] need to control you and I have information that I'm going to act on that I don't tell you about, this is dangerous stuff.

STARR: Well, if you generalize on that, would you say the same thing about people who give prescriptions based on some kind of paradoxical formulation, whatever that means, that that's dangerous stuff?

SATIR: Yup. Yup.

STARR: Okay.

SATIR: Yup. I saw a film of this and I couldn't believe it, and then I wasn't surprised when I saw that the family didn't come back.

STARR: That's not surprising is it?

SATIR: No. See, what is always important is whether or not whatever the therapist is doing, represents a power to them or is this something that forges a connection [with the patient] that is in line with human values and creates a good effect. That's something we have to look at because ethics is a strong part of what goes on in therapy. Long ago people understood that it . . . see, once I put myself in your hands I give my power over to you. And if you the therapist, you the parent, you the preacher, you the teacher, you don't know how to use that and you misuse that I can be very hurt by that.

STARR: Sure . . .

SATIR: Because the whole nature of helping relationships is that fragile kind of thing that happens in allowing yourself to be vulnerable, giving up so to speak your power to the other person. And everybody, teacher, preacher, therapist, manager has power and they have to learn how to use it well, in the interest of the growth of everybody.

STARR: I think a lot of those people deny it, that they have power.

SATIR: I know it and that's why such terrible things happen.

STARR: Yeah. Have you changed your model or your thinking about families in the last, let's say, five years? Like, have you changed some of your concepts or ways of thinking about families?

SATIR: Everything that I started off with in the beginning is still present but I have expanded my methods. I do lots and lots of work with the body, with energy, with metaphor, with the whole spiritual business. I'll give you an example. In Killington, Vermont two weeks ago I was [doing therapy] with a man and a woman. At a certain point in time I was asking the man what he wanted to have happen and I noticed he became very tight, very tight, and it was just subtle but it was there. His wife was responding. I asked him for some response and that tightness got greater. I said to him, "Can you tell me what's going on inside you." He said, "it hurts." I said, "Can you give me a picture?" He said, "Yes, like a big, black thing." He made this kind of movement. So I said to him, "Can you go further?" He said, "No, I can't." So I said, "Would you allow me to give you my hand and will you put your hand in my hand and tell my hand through your hand what's happening for you?"

STARR: What'd he do?

SATIR: And he did. And then I said to him, "Let's play back the message I got," and the message that I got from you was, "I'm feeling like a very little boy and in my growing up if I didn't know the right answer I would be beaten." I said, "is that true?" He said, "Yes." I said, "Keep in my hand and feel my hand now to see what that's going to be," and within moments it all began to flow. Alright. I hear you go on when you don't know how to do that. Now, what does that mean? It means that I'm much more aware now of the total ways in which people express themselves; through their hands, through their feet, through their eyes, through their looks. I'm reminded of when I was in Prague a few years ago. I was invited to go to a home for retarded children. These children were all sitting in their bags, their baskets, sitting like this and some of them were fourteen years old so I just went with my hand . . . Let me have your hand for a minute and just do like so. [Demonstrates]

STARR: Like this?

SATIR: Yeah. Like this. Okay. You see what you have to do with your face?

STARR: I have to contort my face.

SATIR: So I just went up like that and I put my other hand on and I just waited for them to respond, in fact, I didn't pull or anything. These nurses were around me and they looked at me and said, "That child has never unfolded her hands. And look, there's light in her eyes." I said, "Yes." I spent the rest of the time teaching them [the nurses] how to touch. You see I, what has helped me is I deal with so many people who are deaf or blind, who don't speak the same language as myself, and who come from many different walks of life. What has been upper-most with me is how to make meaning. Words are such a [poor] way of making meaning. To me they are a measure to affirm meaning, but that's really not where meaning is made. And when you have somebody who can't see, somebody who can't hear, somebody whose language is totally different . . . I've learned that out of all this that whether you're blind or deaf or can't talk you make the meaning through your body and through your vibrations. And so it's a natural thing now, more natural for me to find all kinds of different ways to put meaning to words people are using, but that's not all there is. And I just know what human beings have in the way of possibilities. But as a therapist I'm much more, much more into the different channels of how people make meaning.

STARR: Sure. That sounds great. What did the nurses do? Did they look at you as though you were crazy?

SATIR: At first they did, it was that thing . . . [pause] you might have seen this before where somebody is awed, awed at what they've seen. Now awe usually creates a fear and it creates an excitement. So I often have that with families, that they get awed about what might happen. I think of many, many, many years ago in Chicago when I interviewed a family where the little boy hadn't talked. He was twelve years old. I interviewed the family for two hours on-stage in front of five hundred people and this boy was talking at the end.

STARR: The boy was an elective mute?-

SATIR: He didn't talk.

STARR: He never talked in his life?

SATIR: No, and by that time he was talking up a brainstorm.

STARR: Really? That must have been unbelievable.

SATIR: It was unbelievable. People that . . . It really wasn't unbelievable because see, what's the point of saying anything if you're not going to be listened to and that's what it came to.

STARR: It was that simple?

SATIR: See, most things *are* simple. It's only how we get down to it. How we get down to it is a lot more than that because it was a whole tight thing between his mother and father. What I worked on was between them. But anyway, Maya Angelou in her book, *I Know Why The Caged Bird Sings,* talks about how she was mute for two years because she was attacked by the uncle, her father found out about it and—

STARR: You mean sexually attacked?

SATIR: Sexually attacked. Her father found out about it through her having told her grandmother. Grandmother told the father, the father went out and killed the uncle. So she got the idea that her mouth killed people. She shut up for two years and she didn't say a word to anybody. Mute. Alright, her grandmother got her to talk by getting her to sing and helping her to deal with all this. See, what I find the more I go [into these things] is that everything is understandable. We just have to find out how.

STARR: That's a fascinating story because people who stutter don't when they sing.

SATIR: Um huh.

STARR: Right, that's a known fact.

SATIR: Yup. Don't want to. But anyway, so when you ask one that question that's where it is. And I see we're into the possibility like in the book, *The Family Unconscious,* into being aware of things that influence us which are not able to be, that you can't touch like family myths, and family treasures of different sorts, psychological ones, and heritages from the past, all that is present through energies I think.

Virginia Satir's Spirituality

Barbara Jo Brothers

SUMMARY. A brief analysis of Virginia Satir's philosophy of treatment in terms of spirituality. Drawing from transcripts of her training sessions, this article shows how Virginia relates spirituality, uniqueness of the person, and systems with wholistic approaches to each other and to use in therapy. The article demonstrates Virginia's justification for her emphasis on the importance of not removing "heart and soul" from her work and the case she makes for the greater effectiveness of creating harmony in and among *all* the factors that make up the self.

We are a cosmic event, we are children of the universe, we are manifestations of life.

—Virginia Satir 1983

Since Virginia speaks, (in the preceding interview, "Heart, Soul and Communication vs. Manipulation") about the critical importance of "heart and soul" not being surgically removed from her work, I would like to speak to her rationale for valuing personhood over technique; the *reason* to avoid extracting heart and soul from the psychotherapy process. If *removing* "heart and soul is dynamite," conscious awareness of its presence can also provide "depth charges" for enhancement of relationships.

Virginia talked, in virtually every presentation, about the "meeting of two manifestations of *life* as occasion for celebration," clearly demonstrating her reverence for the Life Force that flows through us all and providing a paradigm for working with any pair of people—father and son, husband and wife, even employer and employee. The foundation of Virginia's work was bringing each person into awareness of her/his own uniqueness—each a particular spark in/of that Life Force. One might then bring the same two people into awareness each of the *other's* uniqueness, the meeting of these two sparks creating a kind of third energy (Satir, 1983 p. 102). This is where we enter the elevator of congruent communication, which will, in fact, transport us toward heightened as well as deepened spirituality while healing the wounds in a given couple or family process. Congruence, intrapersonal and interpersonal, is the means by which life may authentically speak to life via two particular persons. In Virginia's training seminars, one could see her draw the wholeness together in people, then show them how to meet each other . . . then explain the process; all part of the way she connects psychotherapy with the *whole* of being human.

VIRGINIA ON SPIRITUALITY

[W]e began suddenly to be aware that *no human being creates life*. There's no way, there is no way to create life. No one has been able to create an egg and sperm that can make a human being. That's there, that's a given. So what we do is *activate* life, we activate that. And by a sperm and egg coming together—which is the original plan which we had nothing to do with—then life comes. You had nothing to do with how you were activated except in maybe an esoteric sense. You get activated and then there's a whole program there for you. You didn't make it. No scientist sat down at the drawing board to figure out a person, that was there.

Now then, we had to face the fact, where do we get created? That's our spiritual base. That is already there and I look at it as a river that goes on all the time. That's the basis of ourselves, the spiritual base, that which makes it possible for the egg and sperm to come together. And that can or cannot be religious in my terms. You all know what I'm talking about and I think many people know that too. So what we are in—this coming together, the sperm and egg, [via] our parents through their genitals and through the internal, beautiful engineering that they have to carry this egg and sperm, and then we come up like a fountain. And then we do the same thing [concerning the genitals and "the internal, beautiful engineering"] and some more fountains are . . . [made] and each one of us becomes a co-creator after we get here, based upon this spiritual basis. (1983, p. 228–229)

Seen in these terms, a connection between spirituality and the uniqueness of each person, which leads to valuing the self, is clear: while none of us has the ability to *create* life, each of us does inherently *represent* or manifest life in our own unique form. We are each, therefore, of inestimable value.

Therefore the question of valuing of the self was, in Virginia's view, the point on which growth hinged. "Am I of value?"—the question of self worth—was, in her observation, the single most important motivating factor in humankind. Any therapy that was not mindful of this basic human question would be tangential to freeing a given human being or set of human beings from the self-doubt which is known as pathology. Awareness of the worth of self is the direct route toward *wholeness*, the word "health" being too limited to describe the potential harmonious functioning of the individual, couple or family able to answer the self worth question affirmatively.

VIRGINIA ON UNDERSTANDING THE UNIQUENESS OF EACH PERSON

Now, two things . . . My fingerprint, your fingerprint, is the only one like it in the world. There are four and a half billion people in the world [1983 statistics], and your fingerprint . . . every one of you [has a different one]. Now what does that say about uniqueness? How can we compare, how can we judge people with each other? We rely upon that so much, that if I find your fingerprint someplace I know that's you. Four and a half billion [now], 74 billion have been here before—78 and a half billion different fingerprints [total]. That's one piece.

The other piece is, if you're a physician, a physiologist or whatever, wherever you would go in this world you will be able to carry on. If you're a surgeon . . . [you would be able to perform] operations on anyone because heads stay on the top, feet on the bottom, hearts are about right here—relationship of parts is the same. However, each *part* is unique. No femur bone is exatly like another femur bone. You know it by its general characteristics. No pair of eyes is exactly the same. When you really get into that then, you can see the base for how you are unique. But we would be in a funny space if we didn't also have guaranteed sameness and *the sameness is the relationship between the parts.*

Now all this is relatively new, and we turn to people [like] Lao-Tzu. We turn to philosophers, to Buddha, to Christ—because those people knew something about that [sameness being the relationship between the parts]. And I think the world wasn't ready to hear it until now . . .

. . . Now then, what you're having now is a revival come in a new form. It's called *being in touch with yourself*, it's called valuing yourself, it's called understanding how you work—because, 'Know yourself,' usually meant, in the past, 'Know what's bad with you,' instead of 'How do all these things work?' '' (1983, p. 229–230)

Virginia's point was that one would practically be *forced* to value oneself if one thought seriously about the particular construction of one's fingertip never having existed before in the entire history of the world. It is an undeniable picture of utter uniqueness, a clear invitation to self-appreciation.

Speaking to "the relationship between the parts," Virginia appreciated systems in a comprehensive way, describing all the components of a given human being's system as that person's set of "universal personal resources" (1991, p. 275). Leading the person toward access of those inherent resources would be of infinitely more value and expediency than focusing on solving problems one by one. With access to the universal personal resources, the power is in the *patient*. Therapies that feature manipulation leave the power in the therapist.

VIRGINIA ON WHOLENESS

Virginia was fond of using that "river of life" imagery to convey the concepts of wholeness and connectedness. Following this train of connection-making we have boarded, we see that Virginia had developed an eight point description of the "I," point one being the body and point eight being "the spiritual—the life force." Starting at the point of our senses being "holes" or "channels" through which information enters our bodies, she made connection between "hole-iness" (full use of the senses and full functioning of the glands which are internal senses), wholeness (the putting together of the eight aspects of the "self mandala," those eight universal personal resources), and holiness (connecting back to the spiritual). She would go on to *apply* this wholeness idea so beautifully to the therapy process. Whole "selves" are in a far better position to fully meet the "other"; this is the reason Virginia would always start with the personhood of each of the individuals whether she worked with an individual, family or couple.

These eight factors may be described as a "picture of a system diagnosis," as "universal personal resources" or as the spiral of the "self mandala" (Satir 1991, p. 274–279):

1. the body, the physical;
2. the intellectual;
3. the emotional;
4. the sensual;

5. the interactional;
6. the nutritional;
7. the contextual;
8. the spiritual—the life-force.

Obviously, the division of the eight into list form is arbitrary; it is quite clear that there can be no "sensual aspect" or "nutritional aspect" without a body to contain it, etc. However, humankind has behaved as if the eight *were* divisible. According to Virginia: historically, we put the spiritual in the hands of religion, permitted only the people in the performing arts to make use of the sensual (learn about use of voice, etc.), behaved as though the contextual did not exist, ignored the implications of the nutritional, only paid attention to the interactional in terms of bad behavior, related the emotional to morality, and left the physical and the intellectual in the hands of physicians and teachers respectively. "And none of those people spoke to each other" (Satir 1983 p. 260–261).

Virginia's broad vision saw the possibility of wholeness in remembering to consider *all eight factors* in working with families, individuals or couples—as well as maintaining a check on one's own state of harmony or disharmony.

My picture: If . . . all these parts were known to us and accepted by us, we would have a *spiral of all these things together* . . .

. . . We would never forget that they're all connected to something else. So that the *eight* questions I would ask myself when something happens is (1) Where am I in my feeling of love for my life-force? (2) Where am I in terms of what I've been eating? (3) Where am I in terms of what I've been thinking? (4) What I have been feeling? (5) What my body is doing? (6) What have been my interactions with people?

And I could begin to take a self-administered inventory of helping me to be where I was. Add up negative use of all that and you get stress which kills. That is what stress is about. These things [the eight] don't work harmoniously. Why? [Example reasons:] There is a thought I can't bear, there's a situation I don't want the way that it is, or whatever. (Satir, 1983, p. 270–271)

To bring out the point that all divisions of these factors are artificial, she speaks to the *connectedness* of feeling/body/mind/soul:

We are really all strung together. We are the outcome of our thoughts, how we perceive, our feelings, all our body processes, our life-force and all our behaviors. They are all strung together. Everything makes sense [although it may not] necessarily [be] comfortable. Thoughts influence feelings, feelings influence the body processes, this relates to the life-force, to our behavior. Our behavior influences our life-force, our body processes create feelings and out of that we get some thoughts about it. We get some feelings and that influences our body, then we get thoughts about it and we go to our life-force and our behaviors. We are all mixed up like that. There are not steps one right after the other. It's all a whole, round thing . . . (Satir, 1982)

Virginia's thinking seems to be similar to that of Pierre Teilhard de Chardin in terms of human connectedness as evolutionary resource, with the idea that humanity may evolve—through making deep connections with each other—toward cooperative activity rather than toward the dominance/submission model which has pervaded humankind with so much destructive impact.
Teilhard:

As I pointed out, for one form of synthesis that brings freedom there are hundreds of others that lead only to the vilest forms of bondage. We are only too conscious of this; but how can we come together *in such a way as to free ourselves*? In virtue of the laws of moleculization, the problem obviously consists in finding the way of grouping ourselves together not 'tangentially,' in the nexus of an extrinsic activity or function, but 'radially,' *centre to centre*; how to associate in such a way as, by synthesis, to stimulate deep within ourselves a progress that is directly *centric* in nature. In other words, what we have to do is to love one another—because love is equally by definition the name we give to 'inter-centric' actions. By its nature, love is the only synthesizing energy whose differentiating action can super-personalize us. (Teilhard 1963, p. 47)

Recognizing love alone as not enough, the *groundwork* is laid for love to flourish by (a) teaching the *process* of how each self may learn to center her/his self and obtain access to one's inner resources; (b) teaching the process by which these two centered beings may then make congruent connection. In this way, Virginia *embodied* that which the philosophers describe.

Always making use of colorful metaphor and analogy, Virginia summarizes this process: Holey > wholey > holy

When we release the energy of the holes we become 'wholey.' . . . the eyes and the ears and the mouth and the skin and the taste are external sensors for bringing things in . . . canals, holes . . .'' (1983, p. 254)

Releasing the energy of these ''holes'' is, literally, coming back to our senses, relinquishing the restriction we learned in childhood: Don't look, don't listen, don't touch, don't taste, don't smell. Taking back access and releasing the energy in the use of our senses, including the ''internal sensing'' done by the glands in our bodies, is the route toward becoming whole.

There are plenty of people that are adjusted to the loss of their holes. They don't even know what they would be like if they had them. So one of our other opportunities is to help to awaken how the world could be if we were in touch totally with our freedoms to see, to hear, to smell, to taste, to touch . . . *And since that is the chief and only connection to the outside, our sense, it is essential that we have them in order* [italics mine]. (1983, p. 250)

This understanding of what one might have thought to be the obvious is another example of Virginia's ability to see the profound within the simple. We do all know, if we think about it, that it is our senses which connect us to the world outside our own bodies. However, *Virginia* is the first therapist to take seriously these basics in her contribution to the psycho-therapy world as she put together her unique "ingredients for an interaction," and concept of congruent communication (Brothers 1987, 1988, 1990, 1991; Satir 1991, p. 65–84 & 121–145) having made careful clinical observation of human com-munication in thousands of families over a period of more than 50 years.

Thus any form of therapy which ignores *any* segment of the eightfold nature of the human systems will be limited. Whether one is engaged in individual, family or couples therapy, not acknowledging heart and soul opens the door to manipulation and power plays. The reason for not leaving "heart and soul" out of the therapy process is because to do so is to neglect the very essence of what makes the human being *be*. So much more is possible in looking at the *whole* picture. So much more energy can be activated when the *eight* factors that form the spiral of the self are brought into harmony.

Look deeply enough, look with opened eyes, and we do see the holy . . .

And when we bring wholey together manifested, we become "holy." (Satir 1983, p. 250)

REFERENCES

Brothers, B. J. (1987a). "Independence" *avoids* intimacy: Avoidance of intimacy kills. *VOICES: The Art and Science of Psychotherapy 23*(1), 10–23.

Brothers, B. J. (1987b). "Bless Me, Father, for I have sinned" or: "Wake me mother, when you rise . . . , *VOICES: The Art and Science of Psychotherapy, 23*(3), pp. 12–19.

Brothers, B. J. (1988a). The cancer patient is the self-contained patient. *The Psychotherapy Patient 4*(3/4), 227–241.

Brothers, B. J. (1988b). Remorse and Regeneration. *The Psychotherapy Patient, 5*(1/2), 47–62.

Brothers, B. J. (1990). Self-Esteem and congruent communication: Virginia Satir's road to integration, *Advanced Development: a Journal on Adult Giftedness, Vol. 2.*

Brothers, B. J. (1991). Methods for connectedness: Virginia Satir's contribution to the process of human communication, *Journal of Couples Therapy,* Vol. 2, No. 1/2 (1991).

Satir, V. (1982, August). Lecture presented at Process Community II, Crested Butte, Colorado.

Satir, V., & Banmen, J. (1983). *Virginia Satir: process community III 1983.* (Available from J. Banmen, Delta Psychological Associates, Inc., 11213 Canyon Crescent, North Delta, British Columbia, Canada, V4E 2R6.

Satir, V., Banmen, J., Gerber, J., & Gomori, M. (1991). *The Satir model.* Palo Alto, California: Science and Behavior Books.

Teilhard, P. (1963). *Activation of energy.* New York: Harcourt Brace Jovanovich, Inc.

Intimate Relationship as Path

John Welwood

SUMMARY. Now that the old external reasons for couples remaining together have broken down, we need to find a new basis for enduring, enriching relationships. Intimate relationships now need to reflect and promote our deeper being, rather than serving some limited role-bound function. We need to understand the ongoing challenges of a relationship as a path that can help us connect more deeply with ourselves, our partner, and life itself.

"I just don't know if I can go on with this any longer," the young lawyer said plaintively. Robert and his wife Lynn had come into therapy because their marriage was in trouble. At first they wanted me to "fix it" for them—provide some advice or solution that would help them put their relationship back the way it was in the early days. But it was too late for that. They disagreed on too many core issues and had hurt each other too deeply during a series of arguments and power struggles to go back to the way things had been before.

Robert and Lynn had decided to get married, as so many

John Welwood, PhD, is a clinical psychologist and psychotherapist, Professor of psychology at the California Institute of Integral Studies in San Francisco, and Associate Editor. of the *Journal of Transpersonal Psychology*.

This article is based on material in a new book by John Welwood on relationship as a path of personal and spiritual development, *Journey of the Heart: Intimate Relationship and the Path of Love*, published by Harper Collins. His other books include *Awakening the Heart* and *Challenge of the Heart: Love, Sex, and Intimacy in Changing Times*. He and his wife Jennifer have developed a training program on relationship as a path for both individuals and couples. For information, you can write them at 3315 Sacramento St. #317, San Francisco, CA. 94118.

of us do, out of deep feelings for one another. Now, four years later, they were encountering the real work of marriage—coming up against all their rough edges, looking at parts of themselves they had been ignoring for many years, and facing some of their deepest fears. When the honeymoon phase of their marriage came to an end and they began to discover the real challenges in their relationship, they felt bewildered and discouraged. For they had no idea how or even why they should proceed with a relationship if it brought up so much pain. They needed a new vision, one that could help them see that their conflict presented them a unique opportunity—to break out of the habitual personality patterns that blocked the flow of love within and between them, to grow in new directions, and thus to connect more deeply with themselves and with life itself.

Lynn was being called on to relate more openly to her tenderness and vulnerability instead of denying and avoiding them through rage and blame. Robert, whose typical style was cool and logical, was now face to face with all his wife's feelings, and—what was more frightening!—his own as well. The rawness he felt with his wife provided perhaps the greatest chance he would ever have to open to a deeper dimension of life. What else in his fast-paced world would call on him so powerfully to soften up, accept his own tender feelings, and expose his heart to the light of day?

But could Robert and Lynn make use of this opportunity? That was the question. Every couple comes to a point sooner or later where they must ask themselves, in the face of the difficult challenges of intimate relationship, "Why go on?"

In previous eras, couples never had to ask themselves this question. The marriage commitment was defined and imposed on them by family and society. The family always chose or at least had veto power over one's choice of a marriage partner. And every couple had a set of defined roles within an extended family, which in turn had a place in a close-knit community where people shared similar social, moral, and religious values and customs. Situated at the center of these wider networks, marriage always served a definite role and function: By providing a stabilizing influence, it supported society. In turn, society supported it: If a marriage was unhappy, community pressure held it together.

Only in the last few generations has this situation changed. Now that marriage has lost many of its traditional supports and couples are increasingly removed from family, community, and widely shared values, there are few convincing external reasons for a man and a woman to sustain a life's journey together. Only the intrinsic quality of their personal connection can keep them going. For the first time in history, every couple is on their own—to discover how to build a healthy relationship, and to forge their own vision of how and why to be together.

CONSCIOUS RELATIONSHIP

What will allow two intimate partners to keep moving forward through all the ups and downs of their life together, through all the sacrifices, difficulties, disappointments, and challenges they may encounter? Traditional marriage, based on social duty, and modern marriage, based on hopes for instant, perpetual happiness, have both led to certain dead-ends. What new ground can we find, beyond duty and hope, to nourish and sustain a deeper, more satisfying love between men and women?

To find a new basis for long-term relationships today, we need to consider what we most value in our connection with someone we love. What are the moments in a relationship we most cherish? Perhaps when we feel deeply moved, or when we really feel loved, seen and understood. Yet what is happening in these moments? When we feel loved, we no longer have to prove ourselves. Something in us relaxes, and our usual cares and distractions fade into the background. *We become more fully present.* This allows us to taste the intrinsic richness of our being—what it is like to simply be ourselves.

Love is nurturing because it affirms our being. Be-ing is

not something static, passive, or abstract. It is how we experience ourselves when we are fully present. Be-ing means actively coming-into-presence, energetically connecting and engaging with what is, right here and now. Love inspires us to be more present in this way. That is why we value it so much, and that is also why it is so challenging.

Our culture teaches us a great deal about having and doing, but precious little about being. When we focus on a relationship as something to *have,* we make it into a *product,* rather than a living *process*—which only deadens it. When we focus on relationship as something to *do,* we make it busy and effortful—which only dissipates our energy. The most powerful intimate moments are those in which two people are simply *being* together—being present, being themselves, and sharing that with each other. Beyond all the particular things two people *do* for each other, their deepest connection is the quality of being they experience in each other's presence.

If intimate relationships are to flourish in these difficult times, they need to reflect and promote our being, not just our personality. What can sustain a couple when all else fails is knowing that they are together *for a larger purpose*: a mutual dedication to their deepest unfolding.

This presents a tremendous challenge, for it means undertaking a journey in search of who we really are. Our connection with someone we love can be one of the best vehicles for that journey. When we approach it in this way, intimacy becomes *a path*—an unfolding process of personal and spiritual discovery. *And relationship becomes, for the first time, conscious.*

Intimate relationships are ideally suited as this kind of path *because they inspire our heart to open while at the same time showing us where we are most closed and contracted.* As we fall in love, we spontaneously open. And this inevitably brings us up against the obstacles that stand in the way of being fully open and present—habitual patterns of resistance, avoidance, and denial that we have developed to deal with painful circumstances in the past.

When we bring awareness to these ways we contract, in the

context of a loving relationship, a desire to move in a new direction naturally begins to stir in us. Our love inspires us to come alive in those places inside us where we have contracted and gone dead. And this creates ferment, alchemy, the possibility for change and renewal. Our path begins to unfold.

WORKING WITH OBSTACLES AS PATH

What turned the situation around for Lynn and Robert was the growing realization that their love was asking each of them to break out of old dysfunctional patterns, and the obstacles between them were showing them exactly where they each most needed to grow. The first step in using their conflict as path was to shift the focus away from the heat of their argument and explore its source inside themselves.

Most serious relationship struggles point to wounded places in us that we have turned away from, and that need attention and healing. At the core of such wounds is an inner contraction against some threatening aspect of our experience. We have all turned against areas of our experience that have caused us pain. As children, certain feelings overloaded our circuits. We didn't know how to handle the pain these feelings caused. So, out of fear, we shut ourselves down, like a circuit breaker. We contracted against this area of our experience, and withdrew our awareness from it. Thus we are unable to be present with these feelings when they arise in our adult relationships. Our wounds from childhood are like "holes" in our being, in our ability to be, to be fully ourselves. These holes are like "dead spots" where we are not fully alive.

In inspiring us to open up in new ways, love also enables us to feel these holes more vividly. Yet we usually try to get our partner to fill our holes, so that we do not have to feel the pain associated with them. When this fails to happen, and we are forced to feel our painful inner contractions and dead spots, we often blame and criticize our partner. This is the basis of the deepest, most protracted conflicts in relationships.

Lynn was critical of Robert because he was not as emotionally present as she would have liked him to be. His coolness forced her to experience old childhood feelings of abandonment, which were extremely painful for her. Yet as long as she expected him to save her from these feelings, she only pushed him farther away. It was through contacting and making friends with these feelings, and in learning to care for herself in that place, that she could be present with herself, find her own strength, and bring new life into the places in herself where she had "gone dead." This then helped her communicate her need for greater intimacy in a way that did not alienate her partner.

Similarly, Lynn's need for intimacy brought up Robert's old feelings of engulfment, left over from his childhood with a mother who had been domineering and invasive. When he felt engulfed, Robert would contract and "go dead." No wonder he was not available for greater intimacy. Although at first he resented her for making him feel his inner contraction, he eventually realized that he needed to be there for himself in this place where he felt so raw and vulnerable. As he brought his awareness to this place in himself that he had shied away from for so many years, he could also be more present to the relationship as well.

In this way, relationship becomes a path when we let its difficulties touch us, affect us, *work on us,* instead of immediately trying to "fix" them or make them go away. Letting ourselves feel these difficulties helps us cultivate deeper resources, such as courage, gentleness, patience, and strength, and connect with ourselves in new and deeper ways. This in turn helps us be more authentically present in and to the relationship.

Unfortunately, many couples therapy approaches are often more geared toward problem-solving than helping two people connect more fully with their being, that source of strength that can allow them to work with whatever difficulties they may be facing. Problem-solving strategies can, of course, be useful. But we often use them to avoid being with a difficulty, letting it touch us, opening to the ways it makes us feel vulnerable, and then relating spontaneously from this place where we feel raw and tender. Using therapeutic technologies as a substitute for being fully present does not strengthen a relationship in the long run.

If we can recognize that love, by its very nature, calls on us to feel the raw and tender edges of our experience and thus continually expand into unknown territory, then its difficulties are no longer just problems to be solved. Instead, we can see our difficulties with intimacy as *an integral part of love's path*. They force us to look at the ways we avoid being fully present, both with ourselves and with others. And in working with these obstacles, we begin to mobilize untapped inner resources that help us connect more deeply with our own being, with our partner, and with life itself.

The Bodhi-Therapist

Joseph M. Rosenthal

SUMMARY. This paper presents formulations and case studies that indicate the relevance of Buddhist meditation practice for the practice of psychotherapy. Samatha-vipassana meditation, the core of all Buddhist methods is described as a training in the cultivation of specific therapeutic talents that arise as concomitants of bodhicitta, awakened experience.

INTRODUCTION

Bodhi-therapy is not another school of therapy or set of skills to be learned but rather a way of being that potentiates the therapeutic process no matter which school or approach is utilized. The term bodhi-therapy is derived from the Buddhist term *bodhicitta* which has been translated by Kapleau (1967) as "inherently enlightened heart-mind." Bodhicitta, in essence, refers to the experience and expression of human existence in its uncontrived condition. The literal meaning of bodhicitta is awakened (*bodhi*) experience (*citta*). Bodhi-therapy, then, is uncontrived therapy done in the context of primordial wakefulness.

In the Asian societies in which Buddhism has thrived since about 2500 B.C., metaphors and teaching stories were often employed to communicate subtle meanings of such experien-

Joseph M. Rosenthal, PhD is a faculty member at Ackerman Institute for Family Therapy; Staff Affiliate, Lenox Hill Hospital, Dept. of Psychiatry; Adjunct Associate Professor of Psychology, Pace U.; and Lay Teacher, under the direction of Ven Lama Karma Rinchen, Kagyu Thegchen Ling Tibetan Buddhist Center, Honolulu. His mailing address is: Joseph M. Rosenthal, PhD, 98 Riverside Drive, Suite 1B, New York, NY 10024.

tial terms as bodhicitta. In the following vignette from Goldstein and Kornfield (1987), the primacy of wakefulness as the
ground of experience, rather than one of its components, is
evident:

> It is said that soon after his enlightenment, the Buddha
> passed a man on the road who was struck by the extraor-
> dinary radiance and peacefulness of his presence. The
> man stopped and asked. "My friend, what are you? Are
> you a celestial being or a god?"
> "No," said the Buddha.
> "Well, then, are you some kind of magician or wiz-
> ard?"
> Again the Buddha answered. "No."
> "Are you a man?"
> "No."
> "Well, my friend, what then are you?"
> The Buddha replied. "I am awake." (p. 3)

What might basic wakefulness have to do with being a
therapist? As will be discussed in detail later, primordial
wakefulness implies an extraordinary degree of attentional
stability and flexibility as well as a freeing up of unselfcon-
scious empathy. Therefore, a diverse array of therapeutic
talents natural to human beings manifest when a therapist
experiences wakefulness as the essence of the therapeutic
process. The traditional Buddhist teachings, recent cognitive
research, as well as my own experience as a meditator and
therapist, suggest that the cultivation of bodhicitta via Buddhist meditation potentiates a broad range of therapeutic
qualities, including the following: the ability to track clients'
process precisely; the capacity for enhanced pattern recognition; the facility to empathize with even the most difficult
clients; the capacity to notice and utilize counter-transference
experiences; and the spontaneous emergence of analogical
and metaphorical intuition and expression. Perhaps the most
striking discovery of the *bodhi-therapist* is the development
of "panoramic awareness" (Sanskrit: *prajna*), the capacity to

directly experience reality as a construction and all constructed frames as open, unfixed and, therefore, open to change (Guenther & Trungpa, 1975; Namgyal, 1986).

These qualities, coveted by therapists of all persuasions, are considered in Buddhism to be an expression of the basic nature of human beings. Without the practice of meditation, however, these potentialities usually lie dormant or underdeveloped (Lama Karma Rinchen, personal communication, March 3, 1990; Namgyal, 1986).

In the major portion of this article, the specific relationships between Buddhist meditation practices, the experience of bodhicitta, and specific therapeutic talents are discussed and then elucidated via couples therapy case studies. In order to clarify these relationships, it is first necessary to discuss the key discovery of Buddhist meditation practice, the condition of basic openness of all experience/reality. The Sanskrit term for this primordial openness is *sunyata* (Guenther & Trungpa, 1975; Namgyal, 1986).

SUNYATA, BODHICITTA, MEDITATION

Sunyata is a term which reminds us that reality is not a thing or a composite of things but a dynamic experiential process "out of which" particular entities and events are continually being isolated by mental operations. These mentally constructed phenomena are themselves dynamic and their separation from the whole is always conditional, a function of the moment-to-moment creative processes of consciousness. Sunyata means that, since every material and mental phenomenon or event is capable of being perceived, described, and understood from an infinity of perspectives and within an infinite set of contexts, no single phenomenon, not even a "self," can be said to exist in any absolute sense, in and of itself, independent of discriminating, categorizing, and labeling processes. Thus, all phenomena, including personal identity, are said to be "empty" in and of themselves of any inherent existence.

This description of reality has its parallel in certain emerging models of modern physics, including David Bohm's application of holonomic principles to human experience (Bohm, 1980; Capra, 1975; Zukav, 1979). It also has much in common with current constructivist approaches being applied to family therapy (Keeney, 1983; Efran, Lukens & Lukens, 1988). Moreover, a considerable body of research performed by cognitive scientists supports the view that experience/reality is fashioned moment-to-moment in human consciousness (Gardner, 1965; Ornstein, 1972). From the Buddhist perspective, however, in order to move beyond a mere conceptual understanding of sunyata/emptiness, it is necessary to practice meditation (Lama Karma Rinchen, personal communication, March 3, 1990; Namgyal, 1986).

Gregory Bateson (1972) emphasized both the importance of the realization of emptiness and the distinction between intellectual and experiential versions of emptiness when he wrote,

> The most important task today is, perhaps, to think in the new way. Let me say that I don't know how to think that way. I can stand here and give you a reasoned exposition of this matter, but if I am cutting down a tree, I still think 'Gregory Bateson' is cutting down the tree. I am cutting down the tree. "Myself" is still to me an excessively concrete object (p. 462).

Not only are intellectual perspectives on emptiness a kind of spiritual cul-de-sac, they can also get in the way of direct experience. As Sakyamuni Buddha is reputed to have explained, even having an ego as huge as the world's highest mountain is less of a problem than clinging to an intellectual understanding of emptiness (Namgyal, 1986).

BUDDHIST MEDITATION

What is Buddhist meditation and why is it seen as an essential process in the cultivation of bodhicitta, the subjective pole of sunyata? Perhaps it is best to begin with what Buddhism, and meditation, are not. First, Buddhism is not really a religion in any theological sense but more a system for profound psychological transformation. As for meditation, many myths and misconceptions abound. The word has been used in so many different ways by different groups. From the Buddhist perspective, meditation is not problem-solving, contemplation, getting high, going inside, withdrawal from the world, entertainment, introspection, fixation, trance or even a relaxation response.

Meditation, at once goal and path, is not about learning another skill but rather a gradual process of getting out of the way of the experience and expression of one's own wakeful-ness. Since most of us don't seem to be able to just let go, i.e., just be, specific methods were developed which have remained essentially unchanged for many hundreds of years (Namgyal, 1986).

For example, there are powerful contemplative experi-ments designed to offer practitioners an immediate glimpse of unbounded awareness (Norbu, 1987). There are also methods for directly cultivating compassion, the form that wakefulness takes when we are with others (Kongtrul, 1987). The most common formal practice of meditation, however, involves simply focusing on the breathing process with "bare atten-tion" while simultaneously noticing the flow of experience (e.g., thoughts, sensations, images, emotions) with the same non-judgmental awareness (Namgyal, 1986). Nothing is sup-pressed, everything is noticed, nothing is held on to. The Sanskrit technical term for this form of meditation is sama-tha-vipassana (Namgyal, 1986).

SAMATHA-VIPASSANA MEDITATION

The practice of samatha-vipassana involves the simultane-ous enhancement and integration of two complementary at-tentional modes (Welwood, 1976): discrete, focal attention to distinct forms (samatha) and diffuse, field attention to the context and to the spaces and relationships among the forms (vipassana). One result of the disciplined practice of samatha-vipassana, therefore, is an expanded awareness of the details and totality of the experiential field as an inseparable whole. One's attention becomes remarkably stable, precise and encompassing at the same time.

According to Chogyam Trungpa Rinpoche (Guenther & Trungpa, 1975), a Tibetan Buddhist meditation master, the "intensive experience of form" and the "intensive experience of totality" combine to "give birth" to the realization of sunyata. "As we glimpse prajna we relax. . . . We can afford to be open and generous. Seeing another way of dealing with our projections brings intense joy." (p. 168)

Samatha-Vipassana as Bodhi-Therapy Training

More than six decades of research on meditation lend support to the anecdotal reports of contemporary meditators that it has many beneficial effects. Among the findings are decreased anxiety and neuroticism, improved concentration, increased intelligence, enhanced attentional functions and field independence, faster reaction time, greater empathy, and a general enhancement of physical and psychological health (Murphy & Donovan, 1988; Shapiro & Walsh, 1984).

Experientially, the practice of samatha-vipassana meditation seems to function as a *process metaphor* for what Csikszentmihalyi (1990) calls *flow*, "the process of total involvement with life." (p. xi) In the words of the Danish philosopher, Soren Kierkegaard, life becomes "not a problem to be solved, but a reality to be experienced." Meaning, value, and a sense of ease and well-being are experienced as inherent qualities of existence rather than dependent on conditions perceived from a particular frame of reference (Namgyal, 1986; Tulku, 1977).

Borrowing from gestalt therapy, it could be said that, as one sits in meditation, one experiences reality as an endless stream of gestalten, seemingly appearing out of nowhere and nowhen (Perls, Hefferline, & Goodman, 1951). Each gestalten, or *mandala*, the Sanskrit term for the innate tendency of consciousness to organize the details and context of the experiential field coherently, has a center (breath) and periphery (all other experiences that "pop up"). As one sits in meditation with bare, non-evaluative attention, the frames of each mandala arise and fall away in a continuous stream of consciousness leading to the realization of the "emptiness" of each frame. This is the fundamental Buddhist discovery of reality/experience as a continuous discontinuity which creates the appearance of solidity, much like the frames of a film when played through a projector. As the central focus of the mandalic progression of consciousness shifts from head to breath, from self-referenced cognition to awareness, itself, a new, non-linear, non-instrumental relationship with the environment develops.

During samatha-vipassana meditation, one continually practices or "tries on" this new way of experiencing reality in which all perceptions and constructions are provisional and open. A meditating psychotherapist, therefore, would remain more open to new information, new ways of experiencing people, and new ways of thinking about them. A meditating therapist would not reify cognitions about clients by casting ideas, diagnoses, hypotheses or therapy models in stone but rather would stay open to process when such cognitions arise, as illustrated by the following case example.

Case Example

Richard called to set up an appointment for himself and his wife Joan. I had seen them five years earlier for several months. At that time, therapy focused on the intense fighting and confusion the whole family (including three children) were experiencing regarding Joan's decision to start an M.B.A. program. That therapy lasted several months during which Richard and the children became supportive of Joan; Joan was able to recognize and put in perspective the guilt she had felt about "abandoning" her children and husband and, for the last three years had been working very successfully as an executive in a high-powered firm. She and Richard described those years as "the best years of our life."

Now, as Richard explained, Joan had developed breast cancer. The doctors had given her a good chance of survival, but she would have to lose a breast and undergo chemotherapy. The following session took place about two months after the surgery.

Richard enters the room looking big-eyed and somewhat weary and spaced out. Joan sits as far from him on the couch as is possible, her body turned away from him, her face a study in anger. I have alot of affection for these people. I am terrified for both of them, that Joan may lose her life, that Richard may lose his life partner, that the marriage, which I believe is essentially a very good one, may be threatened.

With my heart pounding in my chest, I make room for my own fear to join theirs. I give in to the natural emotional process by breathing in the texture of their emotions, allowing it to flow through my body and mind. As I do so, I find myself relaxing, feeling more connected with myself and them, and sharpening my focus, I ask Joan to share what she is so angry about. She complains that Richard is doing all the right things—he goes to group meetings for husbands of women who have had mastectomies and he has taken over Joan's share of the household duties—but he's "more like a nurse than a husband." "You have no feelings!" she screams at him.

My attention keeps shifting like a flat rock skipping the surface of a pond—from their verbal and analogic communications, to my own internal responses, to my thoughts and intuitions about what is going on. A hypothesis that had been used effectively five years ago leaps into my thoughts: Richard is offering Joan an alternative to her fear and sadness by provoking her anger. In that way, she might feel stronger. Better mad than sad, one of their old dances. My intuition tells me to keep this idea on the side burner rather than pre-empt the process.

I move my chair closer and ask Richard: "can you tell Joan what its like to have no feelings?" Richard pauses, then begins to weep as he says through a constriction that I can feel in my own throat, "It's not that I don't have feelings. It's that my feelings are too painful."

I am aware of Joan turning her body toward Richard as he begins to talk about his fears of losing her. For several minutes we sit without speaking as Richard cries. This is the first time that Richard has shared this depth of fear and sadness about Joan's illness.

As Richard cries, I find myself "trying on" the tone and edge of his voice within myself. I ask Richard if there is any other strong feeling he hasn't yet shared. "Anger," he says immediately, not to my surprise. "Who are you angry at?" "This disease," he says, his voice rising, "this fucking disease." After a pause, "I'm also angry at myself . . . I feel I'm not doing enough." Then, through his weeping, "I feel I caused Joan's cancer."

My voice lowers as I ask Richard to say this to Joan. By now Joan has turned completely towards her husband. I see no anger on her face. Silence ensues, then Richard, barely able to talk, says "I know I made you sick and I am so sorry. I'll never forgive myself for this." Joan reaches out to touch her husband's hand and tells him that its not true. I can see Richard's genogram in my mind's eye and I ask Joan whether there's any other situation Richard hasn't forgiven himself about.

The discussion that follows centers around the death of Richard's parents and the guilt he has harbored regarding their care prior to their deaths. Now I think I understand something new of why Richard has distanced himself from Joan. This emerging hypothesis will set the stage for the next phase of the treatment which begins in this session with reframing Richard's distancing as a reflection of his own unresolved family-of-origin issues rather than a rejection of Joan's altered body.

In psychotherapy, as in samatha-vipassana, the central focus alternates between head and breath, between thinking, on one hand, and remaining open to verbal content, analogic cues, emotional process, and intuition, on the other. In the session with Richard and Joan, I was able to simultaneously track, empathize, think and intuit. I believe the practice of meditation, which is essentially a training in the freeing up of attentional faculties, has enhanced my ability to do this.

I was also able to "breathe in" the intense emotional atmosphere without feeling overwhelmed or claustrophobic. This capacity for radically heightened empathy without cognitive shortcircuiting or boundary confusion develops, I believe, out of the practice of learning to tolerate remaining open, responsive and non-reactive to the complete range of emotional process and primary process chaos as they arise in meditation. Because I was able to breathe in Richard's emotional textures, I was also able to "try on" his experience within myself, leading to a clear intuition about his feelings and state of mind. This intuitive connection with Richard set the stage for a series of questions that eventually led to new information which was used to formulate a useful hypothesis connecting the symptom (Richard's distancing) to his dynamics (his guilt about letting loved ones down when they are seriously ill). The new hypothesis then led to the reframe intervention which broke the vicious cycle of hurt and anger. The couple were then able to move forward together collaboratively, facing the very real challenges posed by Joan's illness.

MEDITATION, ATTENTION, THERAPY

The central role of attention in human life was one of the key Principles of Psychology proposed by William James in 1890. James wrote that,

> {T}he practical and theoretical life of whole species, as well as of individual beings, results from the selection which the habitual direction of their attention involves . . . {E}ach of us literally chooses, by his ways of attending to things, what sort of universe he shall appear to himself to inhabit. (p. 424)

James went on to state that the educational program that could enhance attentional faculties would be "the education par excellence." James performed certain informal experiments on the cultivation of attention with himself as subject and, after a short while, came to the pessimistic conclusion that attention was barely susceptible to training. Anecdotal reports of hundreds of thousands of meditation practitioners over the last twenty-five hundred years, as well as a growing body of recent research indicates that, James' limited experiments notwithstanding, meditators do, indeed, develop extraordinary attentional capacities (Murphy & Donovan, 1988; Shapiro & Walsh, 1984).

AWAKENED BY EVERYTHING

As the bodhi-therapist learns in meditation to trust uncontrived attention and perception, the world becomes more interesting. According to the great zen master Dogen,

> To study the Buddha way is to study the self.
> To study the self is to forget the self.
> To forget the self is to become awakened by Everything.
> (Kim, 1975, p. 160)

To become awakened by everything. What might this mean for a bodhi-therapist? As the bodhi-therapist "studies" the "self" in meditation, he or she "forgets" the self by realizing its provisional, "empty" essence. Uncontrived attention and perception become invested with more energy as they are freed from a "self-centered" context. Everything becomes more inherently interesting as perception is no longer filtered exclusively through the instrumental lens of a "self."

As the meditator-therapist's attention and perception become more invested with energy, even clients become more interesting, more human, not experienced as problems or adversaries. With enhanced attention, more and more subtle bits of relevant, perhaps crucial information (the essential ingredient for any brand of therapy) become observed and integrated into the evolving pattern of the therapist's hypotheses. The master hypnotist and strategic therapist, Milton Erickson, put it quite succinctly: "when you want to find things out about your patients, observe (O'Hanlon, 1987, p. 14)." In the following example, uncontrived observation leads to a natural curiosity which elicits information useful in understanding a couples' interpersonal dynamics.

Case Example

Clients usually telegraph useful information right from the start of therapy. Its almost as if they are saying, "Look, here is a clue. I can't tell you directly what's going on but if you look closely, you'll get it." A gay couple, Philip and Victor, came to see me because of their fighting. Victor was beginning to show symptoms related to his having been infected with HIV, the virus associated with AIDS. Victor came to the session with a book bag and a book falling out of it as he placed it on the floor. I said, "That looks like an interesting book. What is it?" It turned out to be a book about alcoholism that Victor had seen on his doctor's shelf when he went for treatment for his HIV syndrome. At Victor's request, the doctor had loaned it to him. The image of a young man with HIV illness searching his doctor's shelf not for a book on the immune system or HIV illness but about what he believed to be his lover's problem, was a precise metaphor for the complementary couple's dance that helped me to understand the presenting problem. This metaphor emerged from a natural curiosity about my client's choice of books rather than from a fixation about developing a hypothesis.

In the case of Victor and Philip, I believe that the emergence of the couple's dance hypothesis in the spontaneous way that it did was a factor that boosted the power of my reframing their presenting problem. From the genogram I learned that Victor had been his younger sister's caretaker until the time he met Philip, five years before the therapy session. A discussion of Philip's family history revealed that his mother had given him up as an infant, felt enormous guilt, and then taken him back several years later. Philip then "offered himself" to his mother in his teens as a "bad boy" so that she might have the opportunity to successfully reparent him. I reframed Philip's drinking as a loving way to help Victor stay strong and in a familiar role even in the face of his illness, not having to focus on his own vulnerability. I ended the reframe by saying, "The amount you drink is clearly not healthy for you, Philip. You abuse your body and keep your life on hold. I don't know if I could make that kind of sacrifice for someone I loved." I really meant it. I *felt* Philip's bad boy behavior as his way of loving first his mother, and then his lover. As the therapy unfolded with this reframe as its central thread, Philip's drinking became less of an issue. The intense fighting stopped. Philip, who was an interior decorator, created a beautiful healing environment for Victor in their apartment and lovingly cared for him until Victor's death about a year later. Philip then organized a beautiful memorial service in Victor's honor.

As the case examples indicate, wakefulness does not imply the inability to think but that cognition does not become reified. "You can experience a sense of existence, or being, that includes your thoughts, but is not conditioned by your thoughts or limited to your thinking process" (Trungpa, 1984, p. 67). Contrary to some popular misconceptions, the goal of meditation is not to supplant the intellect but to free it from the constrictions that limit its full potential.

Case Example

A couple came in for marital therapy. The woman complained that her husband was so controlling that it was ruining their marriage. I asked for examples. She said that he always bothers her when she is in the kitchen by hanging around and telling her how to do things. I said, "Are you sure you don't mean lonely rather than controlling?" They both looked perplexed. "My guess is that he's terribly lonely and doesn't do a great job of reaching out to you." (Later, on the way home, the husband did, indeed, confide in his wife that, as a child, he would seek his mother's comfort by hanging out with her in the kitchen.) "Do you have a soft spot in your heart for any other lonely, controlling people?" She began to talk about her father, his loneliness, and his overinvolvement in her life. I asked her if she could stand to think of how lonely her father might feel if she became closer to her husband. Then I said, "You are someone who has developed such a remarkably delicate sensitivity to the loneliness a man can feel. I wonder how you do this. I'd like to suggest an experiment. Whenever you begin to sense your husband's presence as looming very large and close, pay close attention to how you can tell whether he's lonely or controlling. Is it because you get a special feeling from the look in his eyes? Do you know how he feels from the way he holds his body, his facial expression, the tone of his voice, some feeling inside yourself, or some combination of these? If you keep some kind of record, it will be interesting to see how much we can learn from this."

This vignette illustrates the synergistic interplay of empathy, intuition, and intellect that leads to an effective intervention. As demonstrated in the earlier case of Richard and Joan, the practice of samatha-vipassana becomes a naturalistic training in the blending of empathy, intuition and intellect via the cultivation of attentional stability, cognitive flexibility, and genuine openheartedness.

The preceding vignettes also indicate that therapy, like meditation, is a context for discovering meaning, not from an operational and instrumental perspective but by trusting the integration of one's senses, emotions and thoughts. Curiosity killed a cat but often opens up the therapeutic process. Curiosity comes out of uncontrived attention and empathy, in the space between the thinking and hypothesizing, but only if we trust that space, that uncertainty. The open and receptive quality of this meditative state of mind is captured exquisitely in a famous aphorism of Kafka, although he could not have had therapy in mind when he wrote:

You do not need to leave your room.
Remain sitting at your table and listen.
Do not even listen, simply wait.
Do not even wait, be quite still and solitary.
The world will freely offer itself to you to be
unmasked, it has no choice, it will roll in ecstasy
at your feet. (San Francisco Museum of Modern Art,
p. 19)

HELPING COUPLES SHARE

I believe that true empathy is the core of any successful relationship. When partners share the joy and pain of their life journey with each other, the understanding and empathy that develops is what maintains the relationship during major crises. Like the keel of a sailboat, the empathic foundation keeps the relationship from being capsized by the turbulent waves of emotional reactivity. The following extended case study illustrates how the development of empathy as the central focus of this particular couples therapy leads to a successful outcome. The potential role played by meditation practice for the therapist who views empathy development as crucial to any couple's relationship is also discussed.

Case Study

Kathleen and Ron came for couples therapy. Ron wanted more closeness with Kathleen. Kathleen said she could not get through to Ron. "I want someone to take care of me and Ron won't do it." Kathleen is a social worker who had recently started a very successful and time-demanding consultation service. Ron works in sales. They have been married for ten years. She is 57, he 64. Kathleen had never been married. Ron was divorced with two grown sons when the couple met twelve years before.

In the first session, both described their childhoods, Kathleen as the parentified oldest child of three, Ron as the scapegoated younger brother of the family "hero." One focus of the session was the long, lingering illness of Kathleen's father and the effect it had on her and her family. The most powerful part of the session, however, was Ron's description of his childhood agony. Ron's wailing was truly unique in its intensity and the session ended with me wondering if Ron's perspective on his childhood pain would prevent him from being able to be part of a successful relationship.

In the second session, the focus shifted to Kathleen's needs. Ron agreed to Kathleen's demands to set up more activities for them to enjoy together as a way that she would feel more loved by him.

In the third session, the couple reported having spent more time together in entertaining activities which Ron had arranged. Kathleen said she felt better about things but there was still something missing. I suggested some sharing time in which Kathleen would talk to Ron about her childhood and Ron would just listen.

When the couple came for their fourth session, I asked how the sharing experiment went and they reported they had done it the night before, that Kathleen had talked of her painful childhood experiences and that Ron, to Kathleen's surprise, had actually been comforting. In the session, Ron then began to tell Kathleen of his loving concerns for her, especially that she not overwork herself. As Ron talked, Kathleen seemed distracted.

Joe: Do you allow yourself to drink in, to take in what he's saying to you? Do you allow yourself to feel the meaning of what he's saying? Do you allow yourself to be touched by that?

Kathleen: I do.

J: Y-you do?

K: Yeh, I do. Well, I think I do but maybe not?

J: I think you do for a split second. But you don't give yourself a chance to really be loved, to be showered with that love.

I then suggest that she consciously ask herself when she is with Ron outside of the session how many seconds she can allow him to lovingly attend to her. Ron speaks directly to Kathleen of his desire to hold her in his arms when they sleep. Kathleen says that she can't sleep that way. Ron reminds her that she often sleeps holding two cats.

J: You know why. Cats love to be stroked. They don't give that much. They love to receive. So Kathleen is more comfortable with that. But if somebody wants to give to her . . . that's different.

Ron: There's one other thing. Kathleen never had a child.

Kathleen begins to wipe away tears as Ron talks of her love for her nieces and of his feeling that Kathleen carries alot of sadness because she never had a child. I am aware of a hollow feeling in my own chest. In our mid-forties, it is unlikely my wife and I will ever have a child. I breathe in my own sadness as well as Kathleen's.

J: (to Ron) Has she talked much about this?

K: It's very painful . . . . When I was talking to Ron last night I felt so used by my mother, so exploited by her.

Kathleen goes on to share her anger towards her mother and speculates that her love for her niece is just "more neurotic caretaking."

J: Maybe it is just one more caretaking thing.

R: No, no.

J: But it doesn't feel like it. It feels like, as Ron was saying, you don't have a child of your own and you are a very loving person. Anyway, I don't think the cure is to turn off your love for other people. It's a matter of balancing that with being able to receive. You need to learn from your cats. You need to study your cats.

K (animatedly): OK. You're right, cats are really a one-way street. I never thought of it, I mean, compared to dogs or something.

J: When you were crying before, what were those tears about? Ron simply mentioned, "Kathleen doesn't have a child," and you began to cry and even now (Kathleen is weeping), so it seems like there's more to this.

K: There is. I feel like I was gypped out of that. I feel I was gypped out of that because of my mother, of how exploited I was. The thought of stretching myself to the end of a wire where, you know, I wouldn't even be human anymore. I couldn't do it. I just . . . I was so saddled with work when I was a young child. Like I was telling Ron last night. My mother teaching me how to cook lunch and I was seven years old. My head was barely over the stove, you know, and I had to climb on a chair to do this stuff. It's really affected my life so much. It's awful. There's really alot of pain that just doesn't go away. If I talk about it, it's just very painful. (Pause) Maybe it does go away if you talk about it.

J: It's not that it goes away, but it does change it if you talk about it with someone you love, who loves you. Otherwise, you are just like that seven-year-old girl just holding it all on her own shoulders.

Kathleen talks at length of her loneliness and isolation as the parentified child.

J: Can you say this to Ron, "can I be a child with you some times?"

R: I'd love it.

K: Can I be a child with you sometimes?

J: If you were a child with him now, what would you do?

K: I'd let him take me away from going back to work.

J (to Ron): If you took care of her right now, what would you do?

R: I would, and I will, take her away from her work this evening.

For the next few minutes, the two of them plan an evening on the town.

J: How about right now, if you took care of her?

Ron takes Kathleen in his arms. As the session ends, I warn them about going too far too fast because Kathleen may feel uncomfortable giving up her parent position. At the same time, I ask them to devise some experiments to test whether they are ready to make this shift a conscious part of their relationship. I also remind Kathleen to study her cats.

MEDITATION AND COUNTERTRANSFERENCE

In the case of Ron and Kathleen—in fact, in each of the cases cited so far—the therapy could have been obstructed, sidetracked, or, at the very least, slowed down by my countertransference. Since meditation is a training in remaining open to ourselves and others in the face of anxiety or pain, I was able to remain more attentive to my clients as well as my own internal responses rather than closing myself off to new information or resources.

As we sit in meditation, or as we sit with clients, we are

constantly confronted with our own unresolved family of origin issues and our own personal style and psychological defenses. By sitting still and paying attention non-reactively, we begin to make friends with our own minds, developing compassion and fearlessness with respect to our clients' pain as well as our own countertransference issues. We are then able to develop therapeutic hypotheses with cognition and intuition unclouded by countertransferential distortions. We are also able to respond with interventions that resonate both intuitively and emotionally with our clients' experience. In this way, therapy becomes not only more meaningful but also more precise and effective.

How many of us therapists can truthfully say that we have made friends with our own minds? Extensive meditation practice—allowing uncontrived awareness without an axe to grind—becomes the basis for appreciating one's own mind as the local manifestation of bodhicitta, intrinsic wakefulness and sanity. Simply sitting, noticing one's own psychological patterns with bare attention, results in a dramatic opening of one's heart to oneself—an acceptance of the struggle, pain, joys and uncertainties of one's own life. Friendship towards oneself then becomes the reference for compassion towards others.

Chogyam Trungpa (1984) poignantly describes the experience of the compassion that accompanies bodhicitta as a state in which "your heart is completely exposed. There is no skin or tissue covering it. It is pure raw meat. Even if a tiny mosquito lands on it, you feel so touched. Your experience is raw and tender and so personal (p. 46)."

MEDITATION, PRAJNA, SKILLFUL MEANS

In the meditative tradition of Buddhism, it is said that the wisdom that realizes emptiness (*prajna*) is always joined with skillful means (*upaya*) (Guenther & Trungpa, 1975; Namgyal, 1986). For the bodhi-therapist, this means that, like the vacuum state in quantum physics, emptiness is a creative void, the locus of all potentiality which "freely offers itself to you" in the form of an infinite variety of creative and skillful interventions.

Case Example

Sara, a thirty-one year old social worker, had been relying more and more on alcohol and cocaine to comfort herself and avoid having to ask her husband for comfort. She had recently begun a secret love affair. As a child, a fiercely competitive relationship with her father had taught her about the dangers of vulnerability. She came across as hip, slick and cool.

She told me at the end of a session in which we discussed her relationship with her husband and her unwillingness to share her loneliness with him that, after leaving my office, she was going directly to her cocaine source. At that moment, I might have panicked and extended the session. I might have tried to talk her out of it. I might have told her the therapy would have to be put on hold if she refused to get drug treatment. Instead, I told her that I understood she needed to get the cocaine and that I understood that she would do that. I asked her if she would be willing to try an experiment before getting the cocaine and told her it would only take a few minutes. She agreed. I told her to go home and find one of her husband's favorite ties and to get a scissors and secretly make some small cuts in it. She looked dubious, then chuckled, agreed to the experiment, and left the office.

At the next session, she told me what happened. During the thirty-minute drive home, she kept thinking about her husband and how she would cut up his favorite tie. When she walked into the apartment, he was standing in the kitchen and said to her, "you look funny. Is everything ok?"

At this point, Sara burst into tears and her husband embraced her. They experienced an emotional connection that had been missing for several months, perhaps years.

Shortly after this session, Sara stopped her use of cocaine and greatly reduced her use of alcohol. She is now in couples therapy with her husband and she reports that her relationship with him has improved substantially.

Now, obviously, I am not saying that the cure for cocaine addiction and intimacy problems is tie cutting. I am saying that if a therapist can learn to trust the unconscious, something that occurs spontaneously as a by-product of meditation, then interventions often arise spontaneously as multi-level communications that speak to different layers of the change process occurring in the client.

When I suggested this action to Sara, I had only an incipient understanding of why I would say such a thing. After the session, I realized I was speaking to both her anger at her husband (and father) as well as to her yearning for closeness, and that she would probably be focusing on these feelings on different levels in new ways as she drove home. Not until writing this article did I realize my unconscious was really clever in also helping her to deal on an inner level with the spectre of "cutting ties" with her husband.

The essence of the power of creative void interventions is that they are not formulaic—they arise from a gap of uncertainty in the therapist's on-going construction of reality; thus, they provoke a gap in the clients' solidified construction of the presenting problem, thereby leaving room for something new to take place. Samatha-vipassana meditation, with its potential for the realization of sunyata, the essential unsolid nature of experience/reality, acts as a powerful fertilizer for the kind of experiential soil in which creative void interventions can germinate spontaneously.

CLOSURE

There are, of course, many paths to learning to trust the blending of one's intuition and intelligence to create effective interventions. And many methods for training in attention and stability of mind. There are also lots of ways to develop compassion towards oneself and others. What therapist would not want to develop these qualities? The regular practice of samatha-vipassana meditation appears to be a multidimensional path towards the development of all of these qualities, not as separate skills to be acquired but as aspects of one's essential wakefulness to be rediscovered. As an ancient Taoist proverb says, "the way to do is to be." For the aspiring bodhi-therapist, the way to be is to meditate.

REFERENCES

Bateson, G. (1972). *Steps to an ecology of mind.* NY: Ballantine.

Bohm, D. (1980). *Wholeness and the implicate order.* London: Routledge & Kegan Paul.

Capra, F. (1975) *The tao of physics.* Berkeley, CA: Shambhala.

Csikszentmihalyi, M. (1990). *Flow. The psychology of optimal experience.* NY: Harper & Row.

Efran, J., Lukens, R. & Lukens, M. (1988). Constructivism: What's in it for You? *The Family Therapy Networker,* Sept./Oct., 26–35.

Gardner, H. (1985). *The mind's new science.* NY: Basic Books.

Goldstein, J., & Kornfield, J. (1987). *Seeking the heart of wisdom. The path of insight meditation.* Boston: Shambhala.

Guenther, H., & Trungpa, C. (1975). *The dawn of tantra.* Boulder, CO: Shambhala.

James, W. (1890). *The principles of psychology.* 2 vols. NY: Henry Holt.

Kapleau, P. (1967). *The three pillars of zen.* Boston: Beacon.

Keeney, B. (1983). *The aesthetics of change.* NY: Guilford.

Kim, H. (1975). *Dogen Kigen—Mystical realist.* Tucson: U. Arizona Press.

Kongtrul, J. (1987). *The great path of awakening.* (K. McCleod, trans.) Boston: Shambhala.

Murphy, M., & Donovan, S. (1988). *The physical and psychological effects of meditation. A review of contemporary meditation research with a comprehensive bibliography 1931–88.* San Rafael, CA: Esalen Institute.

Namgyal, T. D. (1988). *Mahamudra. The quintessence of mind and meditation.* (L. P. Lhalungpa, trans.) Boston: Shambhala.

Norbu, N. (1987). *The cycle of day and night. An essential Tibetan text on the practice of contemplation.* (J. Reynolds, trans.) Barrytown, NY: Station Hill Press.

O'Hanlon, W. H. (1987). *Taproots. Underlying principles of Milton Erickson's therapy and hypnosis.* NY: Norton.

Ornstein, R. (1972). *The psychology of consciousness.* San Francisco: W. H. Freeman.

Perls, F., Hefferline, R., & Goodman, P. (1951). *Gestalt therapy.* NY: Delta.

San Francisco Museum of Modern Art. (1980). *Philip Guston.* NY: G. Braziller.

Shapiro, D., & Walsh, R. (Eds.) (1984). *Meditation: Contemporary and classical perspectives.* NY: Aldine.

Trungpa, C. (1984). *Shambhala: The sacred path of the warrior.* Boulder, CO.: Shambhala.

Tulku, T. (1977). *Gesture of balance.* Emeryville, CA.: Dharma.

Welwood, J. (1976). Exploring mind: Form, emptiness, and beyond. *Journal of Transpersonal Psychology, 8,* 89–99.

Zukav, G. (1979). *The dancing Wu-Li masters. An overview of the new physics.* London: Rider.

Comment on "The Bodhi-Therapist"

In *The Bodhi-Therapist* Joseph Rosenthal draws from a myriad of diverse and interesting sources to present us with what I experienced as an opportunity to reexamine the therapeutic process in a different yet somehow extremely familiar way. For me the message seems that through a meditative process we, as therapists, may be able to experience and consciously recognize the ways in which we, and eventually, our patients, construct our personal realities from the almost infinite bits of information vying for our attention from both the worlds outside and within our physical bodies. Through a miraculous, and, I believe, little understood, process most of us seem able to form the gestalt, to "put it together" and declare it real. We then cling to this collage of perceived conclusions as a true and immutable actuality.

A fundamental challenge in my work with people is to assist them in first recognizing and then understanding that there may be different ways to interpret the perceptual field. It may be possible, if we can quiet the frightened reactive part of ourselves, to go beyond our immediate conclusions, typically derived at a much earlier time, about "reality," and, perhaps, find that the possibilities are greater than we ever could have imagined. Rosenthal suggests that through the practice of Buddhist meditation we may be able to functionally transcend the grounding in history that, in some way, molds us and discover the possibility of different and perhaps more meaningful and satisfying realities.

I find that when working with individual therapy patients they are often less resistant to the possibility that they could "see" things differently. They seem to feel less threatened by the notion that they may need to "see" things differently if they are to effect the changes that they say that they want for themselves. Eventually, if the therapy is going well, both the clients and/or I usually discover some less apparent way(s) of looking at the circumstances and finding alternate ways of interpreting them, in the hope of uncovering acceptable and advantageous alternatives. These alternatives are not always manifested behaviorally and sometimes simply appear as modifications in thoughts, attitudes, feelings and the like. What is important is that a divergent way of "seeing" has presented itself and may be beneficial in some manner. The therapeutic process allows what is being consciously "seen" to show up differently. This, I believe, is where the potential freedom and growth lie. Perhaps, as a function of the therapeutic relationship, a trust develops that enables both the patient and the therapist to quiet the many voices of the survival devoted mind and to go beyond it. To see that what worked in the past may not work now. In this manner we can help patients stop being what they were, and recognize what they are and can become.

When working with dysfunctional couples there may be much greater resistance to allowing for the possibility of "other ways of seeing" things; there often is a fear of being manipulated by the partner and/or the therapist if one feels that sides are being taken. If it is perceived that the "spouse" is winning the resistance may be very difficult to deal with. A challenge here is to help the patients see that their spouse is not necessarily an enemy from whom one needs to defend. Their partners are people who "see" the universe through their very subjective experience. The process of helping people see the ways in which their partners construct reality, the rapprochement of the different points of view, even within a context of cooperation and love, is dynamic and, at times, very painful. The task of the therapist, at that point in the work, may be to help the couple quiet the defenders within and become more accessible to the process of healing and growth. Empathy must play a major part in this and I feel that the therapist, as is so often the case, must model this for the troubled couple. We, as therapists, are greatly aided in our ability to offer empathy if we are not threatened by our experience with and of the couple. This is where an understanding of our own methods of constructing reality is so important. If we are reasonably secure within ourselves we will be less likely to be threatened by differences we see in others. We may then be able to move ahead.

In "The Bodhi-Therapist" Rosenthal presents us with a way of knowing and understanding that, in many ways, feels "right." It says what I have quietly suspected and discussed with myself about the nature of the world and relationships for many years yet did not articulate quite so well. I found it fascinating and useful.

David I. Perry, DSW

The Spiritual Connection

Frances Vaughan

SUMMARY. The spiritual connection between two people in relationship can bring a new perspective to interpersonal issues. When a relationship is based on authentic, congruent communication the process of owning projections and transforming negative emotions can free both people to love more wholeheartedly and to share the healing journey of spiritual awakening. This journey is an opportunity for growth and commitment to a shared purpose, shifting motivation from fear to love.

An unholy relationship is based on differences, where each one thinks the other has what he has not. . . . A holy relationship starts from a different premise. Each one has looked within and seen no lack. (*A Course in Miracles*, p. 435)

SHARED PURPOSE

When two people share a commitment to spiritual development, the bond between them as a couple takes on an added dimension that can be deeply rewarding, but not without pitfalls. Any relationship based on deficiency needs tends to become co-dependent. In contrast, a relationship that is

Frances Vaughan, PhD is a psychologist in private practice in Mill Valley, CA, author of *Awakening Intuition* and *The Inward Arc* and co-editor of *Beyond Ego* and *Accept This Gift*. She is on the clinical faculty at the University of California, and past president of the Association for Transpersonal Psychology and the Association for Humanistic Psychology. Address: 10 Millwood Street, Suite 3, Mill Valley, CA 94941.

53

based on a shared purpose of the fulfillment of what Abraham Maslow (1962) called being needs and self actualization can be a crucible of transformation for both people when it includes a spiritual dimension.

When a relationship is viewed as giving each of the partners the opportunity to share the spiritual journey rather than as a means of personal need fulfillment, the relationship is no longer an end in itself, but a vehicle of spiritual awakening. From this perspective interpersonal problems are seen in a different light. A relationship based on love and caring for the spiritual well-being of both oneself and the other, rather than on fear and a struggle for dominance, enhances the process of spiritual development for both partners. Nevertheless, the spiritual path begins with self awareness and the journey is one that each person must be *willing* to undertake alone.

Relationships based on fear of aloneness or avoidance of personal responsibility are guaranteed to involve pain and suffering. Dependency breeds resentment and co-dependency is a trap for both parties. A healthy relationship enables both people to grow and change as individuals while deepening the spiritual bond between them. *A Course in Miracles*, a self-study course for spiritual development through relationship in the Christian tradition, describes the holy relationship as one in which each one has looked inside and found no lack. In psychological language we might say that a relationship that promotes the wholeness of both people is not based on the fulfillment of deficiency needs, but on mutual love and respect and the willingness to join without defensiveness. It demands of each person the courage to be authentic, congruent and communicative.

CONGRUENT COMMUNICATION

When you have become willing to hide nothing, you will not only be willing to enter into communion, but will also understand peace and joy. (*A Course in Miracles*, p. 8)

Authenticity means being true to oneself rather than indulging in deception and pretenses, no matter how they may be rationalized. Congruence means consistency between feelings, thoughts, words and actions. The foundation of any healthy relationship is authentic, congruent communication.

When two people decide to live together as a couple on the basis of unstated expectations they often experience disappointment and disillusionment. If they have not fully communicated their hopes and fears, they tend to become bitter and resentful when the partner fails to live up to the image of the perfect person which has been projected onto him or her. This expectation of perfection may not be fully conscious, but many dissatisfactions with relationship reflect some unmet expectation or assumption about how the other person should behave.

In a spiritual relationship each one may also tend to project his or her soul onto the other. In analytical psychology the soul of a man is called the anima, the soul of a woman, the animus. It is conceived to be the contrasexual element in the psyche, the feminine in a man, the masculine in a woman. The soul is discussed by Jungian analyst Robert Johnson (1983) as a psychological organ of perception that leads us toward the transpersonal and the infinite. When a man falls in love, he projects his soul onto a woman, and a woman may do the same with a man. At first this is intense and wonderful, but destined to burn out in the end, when the relationship does not fulfill the promise of eternity. Johnson warns that when we fail to attend to the soul and the inner life, we become unwittingly ensnared in the dance of romantic illusion that leads to endless searching for perfect love in another person.

The search for a soul mate can easily lead to false expectations, reinforcing this projection, rather than a genuine acceptance and discovery of the other as a unique human being who shares the journey, but is no more a manifestation of spirit than each one of us can be. A relationship cannot be a substitute for one's relationship to God or Spirit or Self. Another person can never be a satisfactory reflection of the soul as the soul inhabits the realm of archetypes. When the soul is projected onto a partner, it places an unnecessary burden on the relationship and authentic communication becomes more difficult.

Reclaiming the projection of the soul is a healing process. In shamanic traditions, the loss of soul is associated with illness, and recollection of the soul is a part of healing rituals. A key to congruent communication and healing in relationships lies in discovering who and what we think we are, and in the willingness to acknowledge defenses and reclaim projections of all kinds. When we become aware of the transpersonal self, many relationship issues that result from egocentric defenses can be resolved (Vaughan, 1985).

Sometimes two people start out with good communication and the best intentions of acknowledging unrealistic projections. Nevertheless, after they have been together for some time they may begin to take each other for granted, and no longer find it necessary or desirable to communicate their thoughts and feelings. When this happens, the level of intimacy in the relationship deteriorates, and both people tend to experience distance rather than closeness. Although this dynamic can be found in any relationship, a spiritually based relationship is particularly susceptible to it if either of the partners is judgmental about expressing negative emotions. Believing either that you *must* or *must not* express these emotions can be a trap. For example, if one believes that negative feelings should be transformed into positive ones rather than communicating directly whatever one is experiencing in the moment, suppression and denial can become a habit that is difficult to break. In a similar way, if one demands that every ripple of anger be openly expressed, it can become an equally destructive self indulgence. The middle way of communication does not mean either self negation or self indulgence, but integrity and self respect.

When spirituality is misconstrued as putting a pleasant veneer on negative emotions rather than authentically communicating what is experienced as true it contributes to distance rather than closeness and can sow the seeds of eventual separation. Authentic spirituality demands that one be true to oneself as well as to the other. When being true to oneself seems to conflict with keeping agreements, negotiation is appropriate. If negotiation is to be of benefit to both people in a relationship, it must be based on honesty. Self deception is one face of denial; lying is the other. Denial, like repression, projection and other psychological defenses that tend to create what they defend against, exacerbates the problem that is denied. For example, if a woman is sexually dissatisfied in her marriage and is unwilling to communicate with her husband about her sexual preferences and dissatisfaction for fear of offending him, the problem is likely to get worse rather than better. What we resist persists, and until we are willing to communicate openly about a particular issue, it does not go away.

As a psychotherapist I have learned that the fastest way to clear up a problem is to face it as it is. If we try to sweep something under the rug or bury it, it remains in the unconscious and is apt to surface in the form of symptoms such as anxiety, anger or depression. Negative emotions cannot be ignored if a relationship is to become a vehicle for authentic spiritual development. Authenticity means accepting oneself as one is, acknowledging both strengths and limitations. One must be willing to risk getting in touch with real feelings and communicating them.

How these feelings are expressed is a choice. Once identified, negative emotions can be expressed without attack. Experiencing anger, for example, does not justify attack or blame. Blaming oneself or the other person involves a denial of responsibility. Spiritual development, on the other hand, means taking responsibility not only for behavior, but also for thoughts and feelings.

Couples who share a spiritual connection and honor their commitment to truth, the Self or God recognize that they cannot live a lie, even if the truth is not what they would like it to be. Trust develops out of the willingness to risk communicating what is true, even when it may seem to be potentially upsetting to the relationship. Each time a person takes the risk of telling his or her partner the truth, the relationship can be strengthened. Whenever a person lies to his or her partner, the relationship is undermined.

For example, if a person who is in a presumably monogamous relationship has an affair with someone else and does not communicate it to his or her partner, the affair can damage the primary relationship. The guilty secret undermines trust, and the unfaithful partner tends to project mistrust and suspicion as well as guilt onto the other. The person who feels guilty usually finds reasons to be angry at the other in order to justify his or her infidelity. Communication suffers and the two people find themselves increasingly irritable and distanced from each other. If, on the other hand, the affair is confessed and the couple can revise their agreements or reach a new understanding and a new level of commitment to each other, the relationship may find a stronger, more authentic basis for continuation.

The fear of truth telling is often associated with the risk of abandonment or loss of love. When the truth is withheld, however, one cannot feel genuinely loved, since what is loved is the facade rather than the real person.

TRANSFORMING NEGATIVE EMOTIONS

> When you accepted truth as the goal for your relationship, you became a giver of peace. (*A Course in Miracles*, p. 346)

In some relationships, the communication and expression of negative feelings may seem to exacerbate conflict rather than resolving it, and some traditional spiritual teachers therefore advocate suppression of emotions rather than expression. However, there is a price to pay for this withholding, and intimacy suffers. A healthy spiritual relationship, on the other hand, seems to thrive on open communication in which both partners feel free to communicate truthfully whatever they are experiencing, accepting themselves and each other as they are, rather than becoming enraged when the other does not match the idealized image.

Anger can be symbolized by fire. We speak of burning with rage, or erupting like a volcano. Fire can be destructive or creatively transforming, depending on how it is used. Anger can be destructive or purifying, liberating or entangling. It is a natural response to oppression, domination or dependency. If the energy it generates is to be used constructively rather than destructively, one must be willing to claim both freedom and self determination.

Everyone has to cope with negative emotions in relationship in some way. An authentic spiritual relationship values the whole person, not only the part that is conventionally pleasant and good. If there is an intention to work together to grow and develop spiritually, each must be willing to see through illusions and learn from mistakes. Every emotional reaction can be perceived as feedback, and an opportunity for learning.

If we are willing to ask ourselves seriously what is going on, we often discover that underneath sadness lurks anger, or that underneath anger lurks fear. Sometimes a person is sad when he or she is afraid of being angry; another may be more at ease with anger than with sadness or fear. Thus a person may stay in a dysfunctional relationship out of fear of being alone. Pain, frustration and anger may seem preferable to facing the unknown. Strengthening inner resources and access to spiritual guidance can provide a sense of stability in times of stress and transition and facilitate the breaking of dysfunctional patterns. The person who has well developed inner resources is much less susceptible to manipulation by fear than one who is out of touch with that quiet center of self awareness. Most of us, however, need help in developing this source of inner wisdom.

A spiritually based relationship provides a safe place for the expression of fear, whatever form it takes. When a couple is struggling with anger, both people usually feel threatened and defensive. If either of them is willing to be defenseless, to acknowledge fear and vulnerability, the heat often goes out of the battle. This is not to be equated with denial or suppression. It is, rather, communication of the underlying motives that fuel the angry responses. When anger can be communicated without attack, i.e. when a person can take responsibility for it rather than seeking to blame the other for it, the spiritual basis of the relationship becomes more evident.

The acknowledgment that blaming oneself is no better than blaming the other is equally important. Spiritual growth calls for forgiving oneself as well as others, and forgiving means letting go of the past instead of holding on to the fears and resentments that belonged to it. A spiritual relationship thus enables us to love wholeheartedly in the present.

THE HEALING JOURNEY

We go beyond the veil of fear, lighting each other's way.
(*A Course in Miracles*, p. 399)

The spiritually based relationship is a context and opportunity for shared healing. Psychological healing happens when two people join in mutual acceptance, helping each other let go of the past in order to live more fully in the present. When old wounds of the past have been healed, they no longer need to interfere with giving and receiving love in the present. When old wounds do surface and disrupt authentic communication in the present, they need attention from both people. If they do not feel they can handle the emotional upheavals satisfactorily by themselves, it is appropriate to seek outside help. Various forms of counseling can help, but one that acknowledges and respects the spiritual connection may go deeper than others.

The value of the spiritual connection lies partly in the acknowledgment of love's presence in our lives as the ground of being and the source of meaning. When we remove the obstacles to the awareness of love's presence, we find that it has always been present, awaiting only our recognition, and our willingness to drop the defenses we have raised against it out of fear. When two people see that their mutual well-being is enhanced rather than threatened by each other's growth, many of the obstacles to the awareness of love can be removed. If they are willing to share their deepest fears as well as their deepest desires, many of their difficulties can be resolved. This can be done much more easily if they acknowledge that the relationship is spiritually based.

One of the obstacles to acknowledging the spiritual basis of intimate relationships is the misconception that peace in a relationship will lead to boredom and lack of intensity. We can easily become addicted to intensity, and sometimes a person will deliberately choose to create an emotional upset in order to reestablish contact with a partner who has withdrawn. The attempt to avoid conflict by withdrawal tends to result in depression and lethargy, whereas peace is characterized by joy and alertness. A spiritually based relationship does not deny intensity. On the contrary, the connection can be all the more intense when both people are willing to be defenseless with each other. It does, however, affirm the value of feeling at peace with the other, free of grievances relating to the past and free of guilt about withheld communications. The feeling of peace and freedom in a relationship is inextricably connected to openness and authenticity. Negative intensity is a poor substitute for the positive intensity of an intimate sexual relationship based on mutual love and trust.

To love one's partner well, one must also love oneself well. We cannot respect another who cares for us if we do not respect ourselves. Nor can we love another wholeheartedly unless we have also learned to love ourselves. If we feel one up or one down from the person who is our significant other, the relationship is likely to be problematic. It is easy to assign blame for whatever disappointments we encounter rather than take responsibility for the choices that led us to where we are. If we are willing to learn and grow from situations that arise in relationship, every relationship becomes an opportunity for healing.

The spiritual connection enables us to see each other as

equals, not better or worse than each other, just different, enriched by the presence of another who is also struggling to learn how to love. The spiritually based relationship affirms the value of love over money, sex and power. It does not exclude any of these qualities, it simply does not depend on them. Paradoxically, when love is present, the issues pertaining to money, sex and power in relationship can usually be resolved. When love is missing, money, sex and power are often perceived as a source of conflict.

Loving someone does not justify staying in an abusive, unhealthy relationship. Becoming a martyr in any relationship is not spiritual, it is self-destructive. The problem, then, is not loving the other too much, but not loving oneself enough. Trusting oneself means letting go of deficiency, need-based relationships in favor of learning to be self-reliant and therefore capable of loving another from a sense of fullness rather than looking for someone to fill an inner feeling of emptiness.

When spiritual development has led a person to discover the wellsprings of love in the innermost recesses of being, there is no lack of love. There is an abundance of love to be shared. It is this spiritual connection to oneself that transforms a relationship into an opportunity to heal the past and let it go, becoming ever more fully who one can be in the present.

In my clinical experience I have observed that relationships tend to become more spiritual whenever one or the other of the partners takes seriously their own spiritual growth. Sometimes it is only one member of a couple that becomes interested in spirituality. In this case he or she may become a guide to the other partner, not through formal teaching or persuasion, but by demonstrating the effect on the relationship. Authentic, nonattacking communication, free of blame and demands that the other person be different can go a long way to improving the quality of intimacy between two people. Patterns are often difficult to change, and sometimes fear of change creeps in to distort awareness and reinforce old dysfunctional habits.

The challenge to love without fear, to let go of attachments and to accept others as they are, is always present in relationship. As we let go of expectations and defenses we begin to see the other more clearly and heal our own hearts and minds as well as each other's. Every couple has the chance of working together to fulfill their spiritual potential. Even when two people have come together originally out of a sense that they completed each other, as two halves of one whole, when they become whole in themselves they can serve the larger whole together better than before. In time, if the relationship is to serve its higher spiritual purpose, each one must become a whole person who chooses to be in the relationship not because of fear of change, but for the joy of sharing the journey through fear to love.

Would you not go through fear to love? For such the journey seems to be. (*A Course in Miracles*, p. 316)

REFERENCES

Anonymous. (1975). *A course in miracles*. Vol. 1. *Text*. New York: Foundation for Inner Peace.

Johnson, R. (1983). *We: understanding the psychology of romantic love*. San Francisco: Harper and Row.

Maslow, A. (1962). *Toward a psychology of being*. Princeton, NJ: Van Nostrand.

Vaughan, F. (1986). *The inward arc: healing and wholeness in psychotherapy and spirituality*. Boston: Shambhala.

Elements of Couple Psychotherapy and Awakening

Bruce Schell

SUMMARY. A basic premise of this article is that the couple relationship always contains elements of spiritual awakening. "Spiritual emergencies," fresh love, and new pain all bring with them the potential of spiritual awakening. The limits in our ability to express love, receive love, and to sustain intimate contact in our couple relationship mirror the limits within our spiritual life. Our relative ignorance of the spiritual aspects of our couple relationship causes stagnation and suffering.

To see ourselves as tripartite beings of mind, body, and spirit necessitates a place for each of these vital aspects within the formulations and actions of the psychotherapist. The assessment of the couple, from a tripartite perspective, goes beyond what most of us learned about assessment. In addition to gathering the normal historical information and an evaluation of the couples' relationship, an assessment of their spiritual history and beliefs is necessary. It is more than an inquiry into their religious history in that it should include an exploration of their intimate relationship with their version of the transcendent. The failure to take a spiritual history is a subtle but clear statement concerning what the psychotherapist considers relevant and patients often respond accordingly. To include a spiritual history allows for more possible directions, but does not impose a direction anymore than any other aspect of an assessment.

Bruce Schell, PhD is a clinical psychologist and Professor in the Department of Family and Preventive Medicine at the University of South Carolina School of Medicine in Columbia, South Carolina.

Mircea Eliade (1958) has written that among many primitive tribes, it is not until the initiates have gone through rituals of initiation that they are considered to have become human. That is, prior to the introduction to sacred knowledge and the initiation itself, there was only an animal or incomplete organism present. The initiation causes a transformation of being. The essential reality that is imparted to the initiates is that they were created by the Gods and thus are in an essential relationship to them. It is only through the initiation, which includes symbolic death and a radical transformation of identity, that the initiate becomes fully human to the tribe. What is it that has the power to transform us within our culture? We have stripped ourselves of much that once had the potential to effect our transformation. We are impoverished relative to the more "primitive" cultures in rituals of transformation, yet we retain the essential yearning to realize ourselves, to become whole. We have lost not only the rituals, but for many of us the very knowledge that our transformation is possible. Our ignorance does not, however, provide immunity from the disruptive power of love and pain upon the ordered stultifying predictability of our lives. Amidst the ensuing chaos that love or pain may bring we wait, unknowingly, pregnant for transformation—a pregnancy which is often delivered stillborn for want of the initiatory rituals. Among the few remaining rituals which consciously links human action with the divine are marriage ceremonies. Those formal rituals, that in the presence of the holy, pledge to create a bond that will withstand the passage of time and the vagaries of fate. Even there the potential transformation is muted through the failure of the participants to knowingly surrender their old identity as they enter a new identity which includes the divine. For most couples the conscious acknowledgment of the spiritual odyssey that is initiated through their union is lost through ignorance. In the evolution of that ceremony the social, economic, and legal meanings have become dominant.

A far greater meaning lies in the realization that it is only in the retort of the committed relationship that it is possible for us to work through our archaic woundings, allowing for

an essential opening to the numinous. Traditionally in psychotherapy we have seen the couple relationship as a unit that
quickly brings to the surface the unfinished business of a
lifetime. It is in this union that hopes are rekindled for the
satisfaction of a lifetime's unmet needs and the resolution of
a lifetime's fears. In that sense the couple relationship is a
crucible wherein there is the potential for the rectifying or
healing of early wounds. There is another level that is also
potentially kindled in the ongoing couple relationship. This is
where, as time passes, with a deepening of the relationship
and with a resolution of the earlier wounds another much
older relationship is intimated. It is at this point that the lover
becomes two figures. The incarnate lover with all its human-
ness and flaws and alongside that a disincarnate presence
calling us to the transcendent. Rumi (cited in Chittick, 1983,
p. 215) expressed it as "the joy and the heartache of the
lovers is He, the wages and salary for their serve He."

The couple relationship always contains elements of spiritual awakening, though they may remain unactualized. The
course of awakening does not follow a linear path. Rather
what is likely is a "spiritual emergency" (Grof and Grof,
1989) that is generally, mistakenly, treated only as psychological crisis. Less profoundly disruptive and more common
than the spiritual emergency, which tends to forcibly command attention, are stirrings (openings) created through pain,
unbounded love, and unsatisfied yearning. Later we shall
examine these more common disrupters in detail.

While the path is not linear, there are common elements
for the couple which include:

1. Coming to grips with the limitations imposed by their
   personal histories.
2. The working through of barriers imposed by the culture
   such as materialism and sexism.
3. Facing and resolving the "normal" limits and barriers
   that impede fully surrendering to love and intimacy. The
   limitations within the relationship generally mirror the
   obstacles found in their spiritual life.

The limits of our ability to surrender, to love and be loved, and to sustain intimate contact within our couple are also limitations within our spiritual life. Whether we are in search of freedom from suffering or of spiritual guidance, a question that is commonly asked, in one variation or another, is how do we know whether some action, feeling, person, or direction of growth is the right one? The question asks what is it that can be depended upon for guidance when the rational known has been left behind. Is there a truth that can be depended upon? The answer to that query is that there are at least three "truths" that provide guidance, but two of them lead to a recapitulation of the past. These three truths are: the truth of our wounds; the truth of our parochial (family) history; and the truth of our manifesting soul. The memory of the pain of our wounds and our adaptation to it creates a "truth" that distorts our interaction with the world. The stronger the early trauma, the more powerful the impact of the "truth" in creating our reality. The only "truth" that leads us to a new outcome is our souls, manifested through body sensations, dreams, and visions. Ordinarily these signals, which can guide us to our healing and into our next becoming, are disregarded in our preoccupation with the logical and rational. Crucial, initially, to the ability to be guided by this emerging truth is a minimum level of trust in the therapist or in themselves. In the absence of that trust, our solutions tend to be recapitulations of previously unsatisfying answers.

Love and intimacy issues are the recurrent challenge within any evolving relationship. They are also the very material that is involved in the spiritual relationship. Love allows us to move into relatively unbounded space, where we are a larger self with more self-confidence, a greater sense of wholeness, and filled with joy. Out of our excitement, we want to hold on to our filled and freer self. This rarely occurs as we tend to attribute ourself-in-love, that greater self, to our partner rather than knowing it is self-manifested and our partner is only the catalyst. In our belief that the origin is outside ourself, in our partner, we engage in action to elicit it from them or prevent them from leaving us, while we wait to again be graced by love. Either alternative is the dependent position of the supplicant and that tends to breed resentment. A further confusion that arises is to see the other as solely the object of our yearning and lose sight that they are also a reflection of the divine. Rumi (Chittick, 1983, p. 201) has written there is only one beloved of the soul and all other love objects are derivative from that. Similarly, all love is seen as emanating from the same source. To effectively bring those insights into psychotherapy challenges us to be inclusive in our thinking and to eschew our native propensity for dichotomous "either this or that" thinking. There is a tendency, when a spiritual perspective enters, to dismiss the importance of mind and body and act as if we are elevated to a higher plane that obviates the necessity of working issues through in the world. Nothing could be further from the truth. This use of the spiritual search, to avoid current life difficulties, uses the spiritual yearning as a defense against life and leads to a brittle desiccated relationship. For example, a married couple, both dedicated to a spiritual life, entered therapy to deal with his jealousy of her involvement with another man. That man, on a similar spiritual path, had become her confidant and her preoccupation. As our work continued, it became apparent that the married couple's search for agape, transcendent altruistic love, served as a denial of erotic love and eviscerated their union. In a sense there was the illusion that through becoming "angels on earth," they could transcend their incarnated form, with all its needs, and escape their feared passions. Both had histories of early trauma which had encouraged their attempt to abandon their bodies for a "spiritual solution." As they have explored their erotic nature, more vitality has suffused all their relationship.

Aba Evagrius (cited in Temple, 1990, p. 31) wrote, "Do you wish to know God? Learn first to know yourself." His words mirror those of many before and since that we must know our personal unknown before we can productively explore the transcendent unknown. The major wounds at the personal ego level must first be known and healed before the individual or couple can productively follow their spiritual yearning. This yearning is the manifestation of the inherent thrust of the soul to realize union with the all. Its manifestation as disquiet, an inchoate knowing that a vital something more is missing, is often "understood" as a deficiency in the self or the couple relationship. The general ignorance of the true source of this yearning has led to many divorces and a host of displacement solutions. That is, attempts to solve the yearning through objects that are not the true object of the yearning and hence are inherently unable to fully satisfy. These solutions in that they provide partial satisfaction to a vital need but never totally satisfy it are liable to become addictive. This may be seen in the commonly accepted addictions of drugs and alcohol and in its more subtle form as addiction to wealth, power, or the perfect relationship. Some addictions, perhaps all, represent a failed solution to a spiritual yearning. To place the yearning in its proper context reduces the addiction's meaning, allows for the possibility of full satisfaction, and may free the couple from a nagging sense of failure.

There are three, not mutually exclusive, ways to approach the couple and their symptoms. In one the focus is on the presenting issues as a reflection of dysfunction within the individual or the couple system with an aim of rectifying the dysfunction. Alternately we may see the symptoms as a reflection of the struggle of the individual or couple to break free of their conditioned relationship, their reflexive replaying of their family history. In the third, their symptoms are a divinely inspired opportunity to awaken to the numinous. In Rumi's words (Chittick, 1983), "Every heartache and suffering that enters your body and heart pulls you by the ear to the promised abode. He has afflicted you from every direction in order to pull back to the directionless."

C. S. Lewis (1980) expressed it as "God whispers to us in our pleasures, speaks in our conscience, but shouts in our pains; it is his megaphone to rouse a deaf world." In still other words, "to construe maiming in only symptomatic

terms is to miss its necessity within an archetypal pattern."
(Hillman, 1989)

In our treatment, each of these views leads to productive change for the couple. Explicit in the third approach is that our symptoms are present to awaken us and may be of initiatory importance. It also affirms an essential tangible dynamic relationship with the divine.

A polarity of great importance in the life of the couple is that of predictability and change. The danger of excessively choosing predictability rather than living in the couple's evolving process is of rigidifying the form of the relationship with the concomitant lowering of anxiety and the devitalizing of the contact. Contact then becomes, at best, the smooth interplay of a dance team, which has its satisfaction, but at the cost of obviating change and growth. That is, the couple's future becomes their past repeated. The more dire the early wounds, the greater the temptation to hold on to a relationship by living it in relatively fixed patterns of interaction. The earlier and more grievous the wound, the more time the couple must, by necessity, spend with issues of basic trust. A role of the therapist, with these couples, is to provide enough safety so that the terror of change is no longer overwhelming. The spiritual tradition in its blurred relationship with mainstream religiosity with its emphasis on the importance of belief inadvertently provides a haven for the pseudo solution of denial. Denial serves the valuable function of titrating our suffering to the amount we can consciously handle. Its function becomes malign when external authority is invested in and supports its continued use. In couples psychotherapy, this may occur when the pain evokes the psychotherapist's despair who then retreats from the process. It seems more possible to live and stay with their pain if we can know that their wounding has meaning, thought unknown to us, and that there is healing whose nature and timing we can neither dictate nor are responsible for. I am not advocating leaving our patients in needless suffering, rather I am counseling against decreasing today's necessary suffering at the cost of tomorrow's healing.

We live in a culture that considers suffering an abnormality brought on through our own or someone else's fault. We have lost track of the Buddha's insight that life is suffering, that suffering is natural to life. Suffering, among its functions, serves to demarcate the end of the familiar and an entrance into the unknown, as such it is a signal that the couple's familiar way of relating to each other is in transition. That perspective is the therapist's. What the couple knows is that they are in pain and that they don't like it. The failure to encompass suffering as a normal aspect of life and particularly of transitions adds impetus to the phobic avoidance of suffering. At times there may be more distress about the idea that one is suffering than there is about the suffering. The avoidance of normal suffering is frequently seen in the dissolution of a couple's relationship with the unspoken hope that suffering can be discarded with one's mate. The other tempting, yet sterile, solution to remaining in a couple and avoiding suffering is to arrest all couple development by creating a fixed unchanging union at the sake of the relationship's spontaneous life. This relationship, fixated at a stage of couple development, is gradually drained of vitality and will come to subtly blight all aspects of the individuals within it. The therapist's task is to acquaint the couple with a context in which their suffering is natural to life and a perspective where their suffering, in addition to being painful, is the quickening of their new possibilities. This requires an intimate knowledge by the therapist of the fear that accompanies the dissolution of the fixed features of a relationship. The dissolution of known aspects of a relationship is always accompanied by fear. When the fear is greater than they can contain, there is a reflexive retreat to older, safer, fixed patterns of relationship with rejection of the new and the more ambiguously defined. This point typically occurs when enough work has taken place in psychotherapy that the fixed boundaries of the couple's relationship have begun to loosen and before that change is familiar enough to withstand threat. At this juncture, if there is not adequate support, the threat may be resolved by precipitously fleeing psychotherapy or their relationship.

As we work with the couple on healing their wounds, we are in the process of helping them work through their unfinished personal histories. Central to this is healing their capacity for love and intimacy. Without that there remains formidable obstacles to the deepening of their couple relationship in its worldly and spiritual facets. Primary to this is their ability to surrender to love, to be carried outside the strictures of the ego bounds. This act of surrendering to love, to the other, threatens the pseudo safety to known ego boundaries and carefully created patterns of relationship. It is perhaps for this reason that our greatest openness to the working of love occurs during adolescence. In that phase of life, the ego structure is in major transition as a new "I" is coalescing and the ego is relatively less fixed and thus able to surrender and to be captured by love. While I write the word surrender, the experience is of being obsessed, overwhelmed by a flood of thoughts, imagery and emotionality connected to the other. In the vulnerable, ego, this may produce a surrender to the power of love to carry us where it will or a counter rigidity that attempts to control it. It is the memory of this torrent, that loosening of ego bounds, that produces much of the adult constriction and ambivalence about love. Love is not painless so we fear its touch. It is the disrupter of the established patterns of our lives, that which thrust us into new possibilities and with that has the potential for the maturing of our souls. In the eternal struggle between stasis and a fecund chaos, love is allied with the emerging unknown. It calls with siren cry for us to venture into joy and torments us with unrequited desire. It reminds us at the most primal level that our separateness yearns for union; union with our lover that at times becomes union with the all. As psychotherapists, how do we handle this raw urge of life to create anew? Do we dampen it, attempt to control with logic and reason? Do we trust the intrinsic wisdom of the love inspired soul to manifest itself? Hillman (1989) assigns to love, in all its aspects, a central role in soul making. In this he deepens the fundamental importance of love previously acknowledged by Freud and Jung. While it has been assigned a crucial role in psychological theories and, at times, claims a central role in all our lives, within the psychotherapist's office its role is shrunken. Generally our patients' goal is absence of suffering rather than to be surfeited with love.

It is in freely giving over to love's embrace, with a relatively mature observing self, that we may experience the possibility of our transcendence. Alternately there may be a deepening of the relationship bond as the old ego becomes more permeable and flexible. With a sufficiently intact ego, there is truth in the concept that the more deeply we can surrender to the other, the more fully we discover/become ourself. A difficulty that ensues at this point is that the old patterns for coupling, learned from the parents, are on the verge of being left behind without new patterns to replace them. It is a time of anxious vulnerability for the couple with a great temptation to prematurely redefine the relationship. This limiting of self, this truncating of the couple's possibilities is resorted to as a way to control the anxiety associated with the fear of misconnecting and losing the relationship. When the couple and the therapist realize that this anxiety is a necessary and natural accompaniment of their vulnerable openness, there is protection against a premature closing.

A context that brings the spiritual dimension into couples psychotherapy is where this life is seen as involved with learning lessons and that these lessons are imminent in the couple's relationship. The partner and the relationship then become important teachers. An application is the use of the concept of karmic debt whereby one brings into this life, as a result of prior behavior, certain patterns of relationship to atone for or undo. The utilization of new contexts to understand relationships is in keeping with Gurdjieff's advice, "think in more categories." For some, the knowledge that there is a karmic pattern, that the life they are living may involve an undoing of previous lifetimes, allows for a remarkable freeing of resentment. For example, Tom had been married for 15 years to a woman whom he felt was unwilling or unable to meet "all" of his important needs. He was bitter, blamed her, and was remarkably resistant to any possibility that she was not to blame. His spouse, on the other hand, felt trapped in a relationship with a man who constantly demanded what she felt unable to give and when she tried to provide it belittled her efforts. In consultation with a wise woman, he was told of a past life in which he was despotic, cruel, and withholding; that part of his karmic task in this life was the undoing of that cruel withholding life. As he worked with this over several weeks, he became much less resentful and more giving as he perceived his couple relationship as a context in which he had received what he had previously given.

I have been emphasizing that the couple relationship is inherently a spiritual endeavor. Our relative ignorance of this necessarily contributes to the travail all couples experience, particularly through their interpreting the natural yearning for union as a deficiency in their relationship. That with the resolving of personal wounds, access to spiritual unfolding is enhanced. The wounds suffered within the couple relationship may also diminish the possibility of a spiritual unfolding. In a Tennessee Williams (1950) play, the *Rose Tattoo*, the doctor says to Father DeLeo, "You love your people but you don't understand them. They find God in each other. And when they lose each other, they lose God and they're lost." As beings who inhabit a worldly and spiritual realm, events in one impact our relationship to the other. The pain of the world, as shown by Williams, can cause us to lose contact with the spiritual. Conversely, to be touched by the numinous lightens the impact of painful events.

REFERENCES

Chittick, W. (1983). *The spiritual teachings of Rumi*. Albany: State University of New York Press.

Eliade, M. (1958). *Rites and symbols of initiation*. New York: Harper and Row Publishers, Inc.

Grof, S. and Grof, C. (1989). *Spiritual emergency*. Los Angeles: Jeremy P. Tarcher, Inc.

Hillman, J. (1989). *A blue fire*. New York: Harper and Row Publishers, Inc.

Lewis, C. S. (1980). *A grief observed*. New York: Bantam Books.

Temple, R. (1990). Silence of the heart. *Parabola*, 15, 28–36.

Williams, T. (1950). *The rose tatoo*. In T. Williams, *Three plays by Williams* (Act 1, Scene 3). New York: Signet Classic.

Couples and Spirituality:
A Jewish Perspective
on Exile, Yearning, and Return

Deane H. Shapiro
Johanna F. Shapiro

SUMMARY. This article examines, from the developmental perspective of midlife, the potential interconnection between the psychological construct of a healthy interpersonal relationship and spiritual teachings. To examine this interconnection, several universal themes of midlife are examined: Exile: the slumber of devotion; Yearning: the renewal of the search; and Return: transformation and reconciliation. Using Judaism as a metaphor, the article presents a spiritual map by which to guide the journey of relationship, and a framework within which to practice yearning, tolerance, forgiveness, healing, and return. The beneficial effects of a spiritual perspective on relationship is discussed, both in terms of individual and global healing. Finally, a cautionary note, warning against the limitations and pitfalls of integrating a spiritual perspective in therapy, is included.

Many spiritual traditions emphasize "the importance of human relations in transpersonal development" (Chinen, 1987, p. 123), and see such relationships as important expressions of one's spiritual advancement (cf. Shapiro & Shapiro, 1983, 1984). Metaphors and insights from the mystical and spiritual teachings of Judaism are one particularistic path for

Deane Shapiro, PhD, is Associate Professor, Department of Psychiatry and Human Behavior, University of California, Irvine. Johanna Shapiro, PhD, is Professor of Behavioral Sciences, Department of Family Medicine, University of California, Irvine. Requests for reprints should be addressed to Dr. Johanna Shapiro, P.O. Box 14091, Orange, CA 92613-1491.

addressing these universal issues of relationship and spirituality. While other religious teachings could be used for illustrative purposes equally well, Judaism is also appropriate to this task because of its awareness of the opportunity for spirituality within (and as a context for) relationship. Further, it may be of special relevance to reflect on such metaphors and insights regarding spiritual wisdom and healthy relationship from the developmental perspective of midlife. Precisely because this is one of the more secular periods of human existence, often characterized by what Hans Kung (cf. Chinen, 1987) has called the "repression of the religious," it is instructive to consider whether spiritual wisdom can speak to couple development during this phase.

A couples relationship can be a vehicle for deepening spiritual understanding (diagrammed schematically as line 3a in Figure One). In turn, a spiritual perspective can create a context for enhancement of the relationship (diagrammed schematically as line 3b in Figure One). The first approach represents a view that spiritual wisdom—both about the universe (3a, Figure One) and about oneself (2a, Figure 1)—is achieved through relationship. To truly love someone is to "know" not only them, but also to gain knowledge of the harmony of the universe; and knowledge of oneself. As Martin Buber expressed this, God is not created by humans nor is God independent of them, but rather is "met" in relationship (Buber, 1958). The second approach (represented by lines 3a, and lines 1a and 1b in Figure One) suggests that it is only through spiritual understanding of oneself and one's connection to the universe that one can truly be ready for and experience a deep dyadic relationship. Quoting Buber again, "Through the Thou a man becomes I" (Buber, 1970); and, one might extrapolate, a relationship becomes "we."

Our approach, as diagrammed in Figure One, is based on a systems model in which reciprocal influences exist (cf. Bandura, 1978). In other words, there may be different levels of influence from different sources at different times in a person's life. Relational and spiritual developments and insights have the potential to inform each other synergistically. Using

FIGURE ONE

AN INTERACTIVE SYSTEM'S MODEL SHOWING CONNECTIONS BETWEEN
VIEWS OF SELF, THE DYADIC RELATIONSHIP, AND THE TRANSPERSONAL

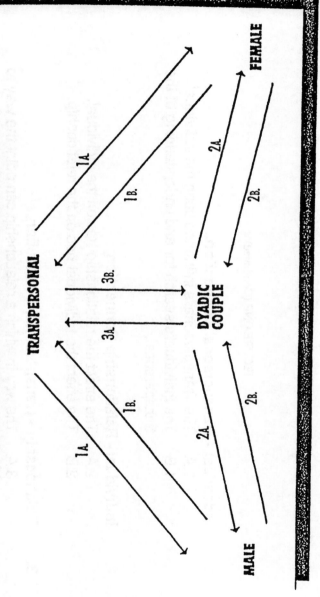

1. **Individual - Transpersonal Connection.**
   1.A   The Transpersonal's influence upon the individual.
   1.B   The Individual's search for and understanding of the transpersonal.

2. **Individual - Relationship Connection.**
   2.A   The effect the relationship has on the individual.
   2.B   The effect the Individual has on the relationship.

3. **Relationship - Transpersonal Connection.**
   3.A   The way in which a relationship can point the way to the "Eternal Thou".
   3.B   The way in which the Transpersonal can provide understanding and a context for the relationship.

this model, we delineate three cyclical stages of relationship at midlife: *Exile: The Slumber of Devotion; Yearning: The Renewal of the Search; and Return: Transformation and Reconciliation.*

In exploring these three stages, passages from the *Song of Songs* (Tanakh, 1985) will be used as metaphoric framework. This biblical work can be interpreted both on a literal level as a beautiful and sensuous poem of love between man and woman; and on a symbolic level, as representing the relationship between the individual and God. In Martin Buber's terminology, the *Song of Songs* may be understood as a statement of God's existence expressed in the relationship itself. According to Buber, it is only through relationship that one can find the Eternal Thou, the particular Thou of one's relational love, and even the Thou of one's core self (Buber, 1970; cf. Boorstein, 1979).

EXILE: THE SLUMBER OF DEVOTION

I let my devotion slumber. (5.2, *Song of Songs*)

As mentioned earlier, midlife can involve a submersion in and an exclusive preoccupation with the values and concerns of secular life. The middle years are a time when many people are most fully committed to their careers, often achieving a degree of success but laden with increasing professional duties and obligations. In this phase many individuals are also involved in building a family (cf. Levinson, 1978).

Perhaps difficult, both spiritually and in terms of the couple relationship, is the "loss of magic" (Chinen, 1987) which seems to occur in midlife. As Levinson noted (Levinson, 1978, p. 102), the structure of early adulthood is based on illusion—the dream. During the phases of settling down and becoming one's own person, a "man must believe in himself—even in the face of reality, if need be." But then comes the subsequent task of "deillusionment" (p. 192). The goals and aspirations of youth either have been met and found to be unfulfilling, or it is seen that the dream has not, and perhaps cannot ever, be met. This may be true in terms of one's intimate relationship as well.

This sense of loss (often compounded by losses on other levels, such as the loss of youth, perhaps the loss of parents) occurs concomitantly with the recognition of the depth and range of our own shortcomings. In youth, the "enemy" frequently is defined as external; the self is still viewed as innocent and pure. At mid-life, all of us have lost some of this innocence and purity. There is the recognition that evil lurks not only without, but within.

We also become aware that there does not appear to be any magical force that can rescue us from the dark places we find in the world and in ourselves. We have become the parents who were supposed to be able to create magic, but have lost our limitless belief in our own powers. From a relational perspective, we are no longer "the perfect couple," but fallible human beings who squabble about decision-making, sex-roles, financial concerns, and "mundane" areas of life that often do not seem worthy of the energy with which we embellish them. We begin to realize that some of the "evil" in our relationship we have created ourselves.

Amidst all these external and internal losses and uncertainties, it is easy, relationally and spiritually, to "let my devotion slumber," to withdraw from the demands of relationship with both one's significant other and with God. In this situation, we enter into an interpersonal and spiritual exile that appears like an endless desert. Although we long for closeness and acceptance from our relational other and from God, we find ourselves isolated and alienated. Sometimes the gulf between us and our loved one, between us and God appears unbridgeable.

YEARNING: THE RENEWAL OF THE SEARCH

O my dove, in the cranny of the rocks,
Hidden by the cliff,

Let me see your face . . . (2.14, *Song of Songs*)

I must rise and roam the town . . .
I must seek the one I love . . . (3.2)

I was asleep,
But my heart was wakeful . . . (5.2)

Yearning cannot begin until individuals acknowledge that, relationally and spiritually, they are in a state of exile. Just like the Israelites in Egypt, it is possible to be so enslaved to the secular that the bondage itself remains unrecognized. The secure and comfortable ways of normal existence, the worshipping of "false idols," the fear of the unknown and of appearing deviant can keep us physically and psychologically trapped.

Ironically, it is often precisely this immersion in the secular and the conventional which can prompt an awakening, a yearning to recommit to, return to, and deepen one's connection with the relational other and with the divine Source. We begin to realize that, like the Jews in Egypt, we are bound by "narrow places" (a literal translation of the Hebrew word for Egypt, "Mitzraim") of our own choice and creation. What follows is a deep longing, a crying out, and a seeking for help in our struggles to escape from exile. We become painfully aware of our condition of disconnectedness, and long for the intimacy with the "one" (both interpersonally and spiritually) who is far away.

RETURN: TRANSFORMATION AND RECONCILIATION

Scarcely had I passed them (those who patrol the town)
When I found the one I love.
I held him fast, I would not let him go . . . (3.4, *Song of Songs*)

As the above lines suggest, the Jewish tradition believes that no matter how great the exile—from one's relational love, and/or from God—no one is ever too far to return. All that is needed is the yearning, the willingness to renew the search. As the great compilation of rabbinical teaching, the Talmud, states (cf. Kukoff, 1981), "Where people truly wish to go, there their feet will take them." We have identified six components of the process of Return: personal efforts and divine guidance; freedom and commitment; masculinity and femininity; forgiveness; suffering and healing; duality and unity.

Reconciliation of Personal and Others' Efforts (Human and Divine. Often in relationship, while we may yearn for intimacy, we feel overwhelmed at the prospect of reconciliation. The enormity of the interpersonal gap seems especially insurmountable as long as we are trapped by the omnipotent fantasy that our unilateral efforts hold the key to restoring harmony. It is at these moments that understanding the interplay of self and partner efforts within the couples relationship becomes crucial (Shapiro, in press, a, b). In the Jewish tradition, one is expected to do one's part toward healing the alienation that arises in relationship. We are not expected to do it all; nor are we required to do it alone. Discovering significant limits to one's ability to control one's interpersonal relationship create a state of openness and "broken-heartedness" (Nachman, 1980), which allows the efforts of one's partner to be accepted with gratitude and relief.

The balance between personal and divine effort to effect a Return of the individual to intimacy with God serves as a useful metaphor for the couple in search of reconciliation. Whether returning to relationship or to God, the individual must take responsibility for personal effort (Shapiro, 1991). On the other hand, the process of return is never conceived of as being solely under our control, nor are we viewed as totally alone in the process. There is a Jewish story that tells of a King's son who had traveled a hundred days journey from his father. His friends advise him to return home, but he replies, "I cannot, the trip is too long." Then his father sends him word, "Come back as far as your strength permits, and I will go to meet you the rest of the way" (Pesikta Rabbati 44, 184a–185b; Buber, 1947). Similarly, God says to Israel, "Return to Me, and I will return to you" (Malachi, 3:7).

This reconciliation of personal and other's efforts has important implications for relationship at middle life. In the formative years of relationship, control of the relationship often becomes a key issue. Partners power-struggle back and forth, experimenting with different distributions of dominance, acquiescence, and mutuality. However, these struggles are often perceived to occur only as expressions of the specific relationship, and no larger spiritual context is apparent. With the addition of a spiritual perspective, the relationship is more easily understood not as the sole creation of the partners, but as a gift or trust from God, the Ultimate Owner (Hacohen, 1976), of which the partners are merely the guardians and caretakers. They are aware of their obligation to nurture this trust to the best of their ability. Simultaneously, they also may begin to glimpse that its purposes and directions are not wholly penetrable or accessible to them. At these moments of fragility, risk, and pain, the couple has the choice to cry out for help, and accept whatever response comes as an expression of the ultimate benevolence of God's will.

At times within a couples relationship, it may feel as though there is not enough energy or reason to seek to reestablish a loving commitment. One of the interpretations of the festival of Chanukkah provides a relevant metaphor to this problem of "relationship burn-out." According to legend, after the Temple in Jerusalem was reclaimed from the Assyrians in 165 B.C.E. Jewish freedom fighters and their supporters found only enough oil to keep the Eternal Light burning over the Ark for one day. The "miracle" refers to the fact that this oil somehow continued to burn day after day, for eight days, until new oil could be brought. In applying this lesson to relationships, the couple is granted hope that, when personal efforts appear insufficient, a "miracle" may occur, and the necessary "oil" to keep the relationship kindled will appear, surpassing our limited beliefs and expectations.

Reconciliation of Freedom with Commitment. At some point in each individual's life there comes a time of feeling trapped and limited, a feeling of enslavement, or that something is missing. Mid-life in particular is frequently equated with lack of freedom. These feelings may arise from obligations incurred to family and jobs (cf. Gauguin, 1937; Hanson & Hanson, 1955; Levinson, 1978). They are also likely to result from the commitments involved in relationship, which at midlife may begin to appear stultifying. The challenge of course is to respond to the need for freedom without losing commitment, of finding freedom within the couples relationship.

What insights into the relationship between freedom and commitment can we glean from examining Jewish teachings? Freedom, of the individual and the community, is highly valued in Jewish tradition, and its central metaphor is Passover. This yearly festival recounts the liberation of the Jews from Egypt. But, in spiritual interpretations, "Egypt" is not only an external place but an internal space as well. According to this interpretation, we are trapped not so much by external burdens, as by our psychological "narrow places." Thus, attaining freedom involves both outer and inner struggles.

Our symbolic relational Egypt is the "narrow places" of our involvement with our partner, the internal Pharaohs that cut us off from our significant other. Passover holds out the possibility of transformational freedom—that by challenging the Pharaoh within who hardens our hearts to change, and by listening carefully to what God requires of us, we can begin to leave the bondage of slavery.

The events of Passover make clear that freedom from bondage is a multi-stage process. After the escape from Egypt came seven weeks of wandering "in the wilderness," with the Israelites continually complaining and mistrustful of God's (and each other's) benevolence. The festival also emphasizes that freedom is meaningless without the concomitant concept of commitment. With care and preparation, the metaphor of freedom *from* bondage can be used to mean the freedom *to* choose commitment as the Israelites chose the yoke of God's commandments 3300 years ago at Mt. Sinai. Thus, true freedom requires commitment. The real issue is to choose well what we wish our yoke to be. This spiritual lesson suggests that the personal freedom we find through self-exploration and psychological growth needs to be reflected back into a relationship, just as the Hebrew people used their freedom to enter into relationship with God through the establishment of the Mosaic covenant.

Masculine and Feminine: Reconciliation and Transformation. During early adulthood, certain instrumental qualities often appear necessary to survive in the external world (Levinson, 1978), and certain nurturing ones are required for raising a family. The literature on traditional sex roles suggests that men have tended to be more instrumental, and women more expressive (Bem, 1976; Broverman, 1970). Based on this traditional model, the masculine and feminine principles are sometimes regarded as antithetical to each other. However, we would suggest (Shapiro & Shapiro, 1984), as have others, that this duality represents a state of exile, and that at mid-life, there is an opportunity, perhaps even the necessity, for reexamination.

In relationship, this masculine-feminine issue involves the challenge of reassessing and reintegrating gender-opposite qualities in the other and in the self. At times, this phenomenon may take the form of sex-role reversals, in the sense of reversing traditional role designations. However, it is ultimately the complementary aspect; rather than the polarity, of these principles which is important. In other words, it matters less who is capable of manifesting a given attribute than that the attributes of masculinity and femininity fit together within relationships to form a whole. From this perspective, the goal for a healthy relationship may be to incorporate the masculine and feminine in ways which are fluid and relationship-enhancing, rather than divisive and conflictual.

In this respect as well, Jewish spiritual teachings provide some guidance. In Judaism, God has both male and female aspects. At times He is seen in the masculine guise of Lord,

Master, King. On the Sabbath, God's presence is represented by the feminine Shechinah, often called Israel's "bride" (Epstein, 1978). At other times, God is referred to simply as "The Name," an appellation that integrates and transcends sex-role dualities.

The *Song of Songs* and other sources teach that the Shechinah is often in exile, separated from her Beloved (the people of Israel), and longing for return. It is believed that the Shechinah will be permanently reunited only when the world itself is restored to a state of perfect wholeness, but that transitory experiences of unity are always possible (for example, on the Sabbath). In relationships, we can hope that, just as there is the potential for masculine and feminine being reconciled in God, so they can achieve a state of unity in the couple as well.

Forgiveness: Transformation and Reconciliation. Recently, the importance of forgiveness in healing "fractured relationships" (Worthington & DiBlasio, 1990) has been noted. These authors point out that granting forgiveness to others is only half of the equation; seeking forgiveness for hurts inflicted on others and attempting to cease future hurtful behaviors are also of great importance in promoting healing. Self-forgiveness plays a similar role in allowing us to release historical wrongdoing within the couples relationship, and deal with present issues as a couple without the encumbrance of guilt.

Forgiveness as a precursor to Return is a potent Jewish concept as well. The ten day period of the High Holy Days culminates in Yom Kippur, or the Day of Repentance. The themes of this time are those of remorse and forgiveness. It is a time to put in order one's relationship with God and with others. Yom Kippur encourages us literally to approach significant others in our lives with remorse and humility, seeking and extending forgiveness, to cleanse the relational slate for yet another year of ascents and descents (Nachman, 1980).

True Return requires forgiveness on both sides. The Bible is filled with many examples of God forgiving the Israelites, and makes clear that this forgiveness was not based on their worthiness, but rather on God's compassion. Similarly, we might speculate that, in order to remain true people of faith, biblical characters such as Sarah or Job needed to forgive God for the anguish they suffered. From these passages we may conclude that, within the couple's relationship, mutual repentance, forgiveness, and atonement on a regular basis can be essential for continued interpersonal health.

Transformation of Suffering into Healing. Unlike youth, "middle-aged individuals have suffered defeats and injuries, both physical and emotional" (Chinen, 1987). While such suffering spans the gamut of human experience, it derives in part from painful encounters in interpersonal relationships. By mid-life, the couple in relationship has an accumulation of both purposive and unintentional hurts. One of the great challenges of mid-life is how to respond to this suffering.

The experience of suffering has the potential to increase a person's compassion and sensitivity, thereby deepening one's ability to empathize with and help heal the pain and suffering of others. Within the couples relationship, the challenge becomes to transform the interpersonal suffering which has accrued into acts of love and healing. This may mean using insights gleaned from one's own relational struggles to treat others more compassionately. It may also mean directing healing toward the relationship itself, to act more lovingly and compassionately toward one's significant other.

Humor and joy play a critical mediating role in the transformation of suffering into healing (Cousins, 1979). Humor for this purpose has a long and honorable tradition in Judaism. Jewish stories delight in gently mocking kings, sages, scholars—even God! Especially in the teachings of the Hassidic rabbis, a mystical Jewish sect which rose to prominence in the 17th and 18th centuries, Judaism contains what might be considered an imperative to joy. "Be glad in the Lord, and rejoice, ye righteous, and shout for joy" (Psalm 32). While the openness of a truly "broken heart" (Nachman, 1980) is recognized and commended, despair is forbidden. Beyond every personal tragedy, every individual anguish, God's greatness and glory are transcendent (Donin, 1980).

The importance of joy is further reflected in the Jewish

holiday of Purim, celebrating the defeat between 485–465 B.C.E. of the evil Grand Vizier of Babylonia who wanted to put all Jews to death. On this holiday, Jews are enjoined to become "joyous fools," mocking the Torah, the rabbis, the Jewish tradition itself, allowing joy and humor to fill their hearts (Strassfeld, 1985).

What do these metaphors teach us about relationship? First, we learn that humor and joy can be catalysts in helping us to gain the strength, perspective, and inspiration to transform the pain and suffering that exist in relationship into healing. Second, we may conclude that, just as despair has no place in one's relationship with God, it is a similarly destructive emotion in one's relationship with one's significant other. Finally, a transcendent perspective can help the couple to realize that their suffering occurs within a larger and more exalted spiritual context; and this awareness may introduce an element of hope even in the darkest moments.

Transformation of Duality (Good and Evil) into Unity. In a condition of exile within the relationship, the couple has a tendency to experience their relationship in dualistic terms. They see the "good" aspects of the relationship, which they wish to preserve and expand on. But there are also the "bad" parts, which the partners wish to eliminate. Judaism's fundamental premise, however, has to do with the unity of God, and therefore of the world.

The teachings of the 16th century Jewish mystic, Rabbi Isaac Luria (Epstein, 1978), state that all aspects of the world, including every human being, have a holy spark of goodness within them. However, sometimes these sparks of Light are covered and hidden by husks (what we perceive as evil). Rabbi Nachman of Bratslav, an eighteenth century Jewish mystic (1980), refers to the continually cycling spiritual ascents and descents of the human soul as all within the unitive context of God. Utilizing this understanding, the couple can begin to regard the various aspects of relationship differently. They may consider complementing efforts to eliminate "evil" in their interactions with efforts to investigate the possible meanings and purposes of these rapid descents into hostility and mistrust. In this interpretation, the couple can begin to view the anger, distrust, and fear in the relationship as the husks which separate them from each other. This metaphor also provides the couple an opportunity continually to seek beneath the husk for the core goodness in self and other. Slowly, each partner can become adept at seeing God in the other.

Repairing the World. Through healing our relationships and making them whole, we can contribute to a healing wholeness and unity in the world. This concept encourages the couple to look beyond the boundaries of their relationship to consider how they fit in the larger world. They can begin to be aware of how the "evil" of their own souls at times serves to contaminate not only the couple relationship, but also their interactions with others, their attitudes toward work, and their relationship with the physical environment.

Luria taught that when God created the world, He attempted to fill it with His perfect Light, which was contained in certain vessels. But the Light was so strong that the vessels shattered. Because of this shattering, everything in creation contains a spark of God's Light and holiness. Part of the task of human beings, what God asks of them, is to repair the shattered world on all levels, from the most insignificant to the most dramatic, and in so doing elevate these sparks back to their intended state of unity. Thus, the couple can understand working on their relationship as a small, but vital contribution to the healing of the planet.

The belief and trust in a unitary God (lines 1a and 1b, Figure One), both reinforces and enriches trust in one's relational partner (lines 3b and 2b), and vice-versa: trust in one's partner reinforces trust in a benevolent universe (3a) and in oneself (2a). It is apparent that the process of repair toward unity is an interactive one; it is through the healing of the relationship with God and the relationship with one's loved other that unity is achieved. The implication is that in tending one's relationship—opening one's heart in I-Thou relationship to the other (Buber, 1970)—one is contributing to bringing to fruition a small piece of God's divine plan—the unity of the Eternal Thou. Thus God requires that we care deeply about our relationships, not only for our own sakes, but for God's.

This pursuit of unity is not considered easy in Jewish tradition. The word "Israel" in Hebrew means to wrestle with God. Thus, the relationship between human and God is not seen as smooth and uncomplicated, but filled with ascents and descents, alienations and reconciliations. However, as is suggested in the central prayer of Judaism, which states "The Lord our God; the Lord is One" (Kaplan, 1985), this struggling with God is contained within a context of unity, the Oneness of God.

Given the complexities of interpersonal relationships, this model of struggle is reassuring and somehow validating. It suggests that the process of struggle, so long as it is in the service of God (Avot 5:28), may lead to resolutions of increasing love and respect. It also suggests that, at the deepest level, beneath the husks that hide the Light, the couple can discover a certain inherent wholeness or completeness in their relationship. Thus, while we can rejoice in the exhilarating ascents that occur in relationship, the "running" within the relationship toward the other, the descents no longer need be so terrifying. Each partner can recall that "Even when I make my bed in hell, You are with me" (Psalm 139), and this awareness can provide a contextual comfort for times of relational drift and difficulty. It suggests that even though the partners in relationship temporarily may abandon each other, at a more fundamental level a return to the other is always possible.

A CAUTIONARY NOTE

We have highlighted the revelance of the teachings of one religious tradition insofar as they apply to couples. In so doing, we have used only positive examples and lessons. However, three cautions are necessary. First, we do not believe that, as therapists, we have a right to proclaim that any person, or couple, "should" believe a certain way—e.g., that the universe *is* sacred and holy at its deepest level (Shapiro, 1989). Further, we believe that there are many equally valid "paths up the mountain." Therefore, even if a person does believe the universe is unitive and sacred, it is critical to honor that person's own path, tradition, and discipline.

Finally, religious beliefs, as any other kind of belief, can be misused. We are familiar with cases in which individuals have been in abusive and unproductive relationships, and justified staying in the relationship based on spiritual beliefs: "If I were truly spiritual, I would be more able to forgive"; "I feel it was God's destiny that we are together"; "God is a God of love, and so are all God's creatures; if I look harder, I'll find the sacred part of my spouse." Therefore, even though we have written frequently using declarative (rather than conditional) sentences these positive assertions should be considered as beliefs and working models rather than as absolutes. It is important to recognize that ennobling and sacred truths, no matter how poetic and graceful they sound, always have the potential to be misused in defensive, destructive, and pathological ways.

CONCLUSION

At mid-life, the goal of the search for and encounter with the spiritual is not to transcend the world, but to reconnect with the more ultimate values which spirituality endorses, feel their transformative power, and then return to the world, to one's relational love. Knowledge of the spiritual can provide a strong and enduring context for relationship; yet the primary relationship also becomes a way of drawing closer to God.

Using Judaism as a metaphor, a kind of spiritual map has emerged, which may be used to guide relationship, a flexible framework within which to practice yearning, tolerance, forgiveness, healing, and return. The spiritual passage depicted in Exodus from slavery to freedom becomes a metaphor for understanding the journey of relationship. With this as a context and vision to help us in the darkness, the often overwhelming ascents and descents of relationship become more understandable and meaningful. No matter what joys and pains we experience in relationship, we can continue to follow the spiritual map God has given us. It reminds us to ask ourselves the question, within the context of God's plan, how, at the deepest level, we are meant to be together, and for what purpose.

It is possible to become aware that interpersonal relationships are at once infinitely small yet necessary pieces of a world in fragments which needs to be made whole again. Inescapably, we experience that brokenness every day through the flaws and struggles of the relationship. But we simultaneously have the opportunity to experience its great potential for wholeness, for oneness, for unity. In the words of the Song of Songs (2.16):

I am my beloved's
And my beloved is mine.

REFERENCES

Bandura, A. (1978). The self system in reciprocal determinism. *American Psychologist.* *33*; 344–358.

Bem, S.L. (1976). Probing the promise of androgyny. In A.G. Kaplan and J.P. Bean (Eds.) *Beyond sex stereotypes: Readings toward a psychology of androgyny.* (pp. 48–62). Boston: Little, Brown.

Boorstein, S. (1979). Troubled relationships: Transpersonal and psycho-analytic approaches. *The Journal of Transpersonal Psychology.* *2*; 129–139.

Broverman, I.K., Broverman, D.M., Clarkson, F.E., Rosenkrantz, P.S., & Vogel, S.R. (1970). Sex role stereotypes and clinical judgments of mental health. *Journal of Consulting and Clinical Psychology.* *34*; 1–7.

Buber, M. (1947). *Ten rungs: Hassidic sayings.* New York: Schocken Books.

Buber, M. (1958). *I and Thou*, trans. R.G. Smith. 2nd edition. New York: Scribner's.

Buber, M. (1970). *I and Thou*, trans. Walter Kaufman. New York: Scribner.

Chinen, A.B. (1987). Middle tales: Fairy tales and transpersonal development at mid-life. *The Journal of Transpersonal Psychology. 19;* 99–131.

Cousins, N. (1979). *Anatomy of an illness*. New York: Norton.

Donin, H.H. (1980). *To be a Jew: A guide to Jewish observance*. New York: Basic Books.

Epstein, P. (1978). *Kabbalah: The way of the Jewish mystic*. Boston: Shambhala Pub.

Gauguin, P. (1937). *My father Paul Gauguin*, trans. A.G. Chater. New York: Knopf.

Hacohen, S.A. (1976). *Touching heaven, touching earth*. Tel Aviv: Sadan Publishing, p. 78.

Hanson, L. & Hanson, E. (1955). *The noble savage: The life of Paul Gaugin*. New York: Random House.

Kaplan, J. (1985). *Jewish meditation: A practical guide*. New York: Schocken Books.

Kukoff, L. (1981). *Choosing Judaism*. New York: Union of American Hebrew Congregations.

Levinson, D.J. (1978). *The seasons of a man's life*. New York: Knopf.

Nachman, R. (1980). *Restore my soul*. A. Greenbaum (tr.). New York: Breslov Research Institute.

Shapiro, D. (1989). Exploring our most deeply held belief about ultimate reality. *ReVision: The Journal of Consciousness and Change. 12* (1) 15–28.

Shapiro, D.H. (1991). *Assessing a person's sense of control: Personally, Interpersonally, Spiritually*. Manual for the Shapiro Control Inventory (SCI): Palo Alto: Behaviordyne.

Shapiro, D.H. (in press a). *The role of control and self-control in psychotherapy and health care*. New York: John Wiley.

Shapiro, D.H. (in press b). *The human quest for control*. Los Angeles: Tarcher.

Shapiro, J. & Shapiro, D.H. (1983). Well-being and relationship. In D.H. Shapiro and R. Walsh (Eds.), *Beyond health and normality*. New York: Van Nostrand, pp. 207–214.

Shapiro, J. & Shapiro, D.H. (1984). Self-control and relationship: Toward a model of interpersonal health. *Journal of Humanistic Psychology. 24:*91–116.

Strassfeld, M. (1985). *The Jewish holidays: A guide and commentary*. New York: Harper & Row.

Tanakh: The Holy Scriptures (1985). Philadelphia: The Jewish Publication Society.

Worthington, E.L. & DiBlasio, F.A. (1990). Promoting mutual forgiveness within the fractured relationship. *Psychotherapy: Theory, Research, Practice. 27;* 219–223.

Holy Matrimony

Stephen Schoen

SUMMARY. Sacredness in marriage is described psychologically as an intense, complex, committed bond, mutually respectful and vulnerable, whose unique depth for both persons evokes the special word "holy." Examples are cited, including the qualities lacking and at stake in problematic marriages.

WHAT ON EARTH IS . . . . ?

"Perhaps it's a joke," you may wonder as you read the title of this piece.

Certainly the phrase rings quaint: far from the norms, the substance, the problems of modern marriage. And here is a professional journal on couples, dealing openmindedly with good personal contact and the projections which inhibit it. What light on these can possibly come from an old spiritual standard that sounds prescriptive and righteous?

I want to begin with a person generally admired today for her motives and actions, Mother Teresa of Calcutta. A student said to her, when she spoke at Harvard College, "Your work of love with the poor is wonderful. But can we, as ordinary people, do the kind of thing you do, with your

Stephen Schoen, MD, is a psychiatrist in private practice in San Francisco and San Rafael, California, and a training member of the Gestalt Institute of San Francisco. He has taught for years, at many other training centers for therapists in the United States and Europe, on the spiritual evolution within psychotherapy. His book, *Presence of Mind: Literary and Philosophical Roots of a Wise Psychotherapy,* is being published in 1992. Correspondence may be sent to: 567 Heather Way, San Rafael, CA, 94903.

special gift of holiness?'' To which Mother Teresa replied, ''It is our nature to be holy.''

Now, perhaps it is this woman's special gift to us who are not renunciants within Catholicism, to speak, beyond any church dogma, of a singular and paramount quality of our inward life: its capacity for awe at the world and a sense of the ineffable in it, its primal bond to the world, its power to be self-fulfilled through its compassion toward others.

Another student remarked, ''Your life is in a sense easier. For instance, it's simpler not to be married.''

Mother Teresa answered, ''But I am married.'' She held up her ring of betrothal to Christ. Then, alluding to the inevitable problems of relationship, she murmured, ''And sometimes he can be very difficult.''

Without doubt, whether with Christ or another, relationships cause trouble. Too much demand, too little freedom. Neglect when one wants attention. Attention when one wants to be left alone. Misunderstandings. Insensitivity. And none of this avoidable. Of course, in worldly marriage there's the chance for intimacy, for sexual gratification, for a familial center of one's own; but at what price? It's well known that people get married lightly only at their peril, but even under the most considered circumstances the peril remains. A new couple must believe in their future together on insufficient evidence, must trust that their idealizations and hopes of one another haven't sacrificed all awareness of discontents that assuredly lie ahead. And now, to add to the risk, the sacred view enters, declaring that we are primally bound to one another, so that in the act of marriage we are involving ourselves—self-responsibly, ''on our own recognizance,'' so to speak—in something like an Irrevocable Trust.

But this greater risk doesn't make the matter grim. On the contrary: the sacred view is that marriage is most in peril if it *isn't* entered into with a sense of the highest possible stakes. If a couple has no feeling for commitment where there is awe, compassion, and contact which is at once immediate and boundless, then at best they play at keeping house, and home is a convenience in which their own depths of being remain homeless.

Recently a friend invited me to a birthday party for Aaron, with whom he has lived in profound harmony for thirty years. Richard is a robust man, a famous poet and great talker, Aaron a shy, almost non-verbal visual artist not interested in poetry. Their common life together has many equitable divisions of labor: one does most of the housework and the cooking, the other usually takes charge of business and social affairs. But what, I wondered, makes for the enduring depth between them? Richard gave a simple explanation. "Our bond is entirely unconscious," he said.

This seems to be the case with spiritual compatibility; we are speaking of something unconsciously granted. But now quite insuperable problems appear to arise. For how can we talk of being forewarned about a relationship, or repairing or improving one (the avowed intent of marital therapy) if we are always, so to say, in incorrigible depths? As with the sense of holiness itself: one can't deliberately arouse it. No precept or manipulation will turn a cow sacred; you have it or you don't. And with deep relationship, too, here is the stubborn truth. Computer dating is bound to be superficial and all reasoning as to how it "might" or "should" be stops at the door.

What rational approach, then, does that leave us? Or to put it another way, remembering Mother Teresa's words: What can *awaken* the sacred within us?

No one, it's true, no marriage partner or marital therapist, can make a good marriage happen. But one can say something of what is needed *for* it to happen. These intangible and uncontrollable things can be identified *after* the fact, if not in advance, and can be appealed to even in a longstanding marriage which hasn't yet given them their due. A list follows. —No, to be less presumptuous (for an X-factor may be present that I haven't myself been able to identify or appeal to), here is my *partial* list.

MAKINGS OF A SACRED BOND

Mutual Trust

Mutual Trust, first of all. Trust is the willingness to grant someone power over you beyond your control. When we mistrust, we put the other on a leash, make him, or her, sign a contract: or we keep ourselves at a distance designated by the word "safe." But trust, instead, has an aspect of submission. One trusts the other, given liberty and resources, *not* to do one harm, to have indeed good motives and inherent competence: as a relaxed passenger gives trust to the driver of the car, a patient to the surgeon, a composer to the musicians performing his work, a weaker dog to the stronger one to whom it bares its throat. In these ways—and in marriage over a lifetime span of years—the one trusting invites the other to be trustworthy.

How does trust come about? It is, inevitably, an act of faith. Of faith in what? In the absolute value of the other person for the matter at hand; and in marriage, of course, this matter is enduring. And as one's sense of an absolute value can only begin with oneself, trust must mean faith in a primal connection between oneself and the other: one shares this absolute value. Here the psychological bond and the sacred clearly join hands.

Trust in the other implies that one is to be trusted oneself; the primal connection requires this mutuality. But personal blinders may enter, skewing trust to be one-sided. The perennially notorious case is the man, with a monogamous standard, who counts on his wife's fidelity while allowing himself transient attachments. The wife may not be unaware, but cooperates by looking the other way. Or one-sidedness may come in a more obscure form. For instance, an engineer in my practice who has had some success with investments wants to *feel trusted by* his wife more than he does: the sign of this would be her letting him manage inheritance money that she has kept, from before their marriage ten years ago, in the hands of a sound business adviser. She takes good care of their home and their six-year-old daughter and shares her small artist's income with her husband. She would, she tells him, unhesitantly use up all her inheritance money to help him, say, with a catastrophic medical need. This picture impresses him. But her admittedly anxious wish to maintain control of her money, in the event of an unforeseeable emergency, constitutes in his eyes a grievous withholding, a decisive refusal to trust him. "As usual, you want to manage me," she has said to him, and that, I think, is her most serious objection. He does not notice that in fact he is the one not trusting her reservation, that *he* therefore isn't trustworthy.

To feel the absolute value of another is itself awesome; in this instance we see the man rejecting it out of his own demand. But even more awesome, I think, is the responsibility one has, being *trusted by* the other, in honoring the trust. Needs and wishes aren't taken lightly, much less betrayed, and the other is accepted "as is"—a phrase, oddly, that we use most often to describe second-hand goods for sale. And yet to be accepted "as is" is to be accepted, without alteration and without design, as unblemished, and the one accepting is accorded a godlike breadth. This is an amazing business.

I want to develop the point a little more. Acceptance "as is" means that there is no more anything wrong with the person than with a field of flowers, or tonight's sunset. On the contrary: that to meet someone fresh, as a painter meets nature, is to commune with him or her unchanged, and just in that way to keep discovering in the person some new quality or shading or nuance. Now, all of this sounds ideally accepting, and indeed it is, so that the witticism of the humorist Ashley Brilliant holds water for us. "Accepting you as you are," he observes in a very careful aphorism, "does not *necessarily* mean that I have given up all hope of your improving." And yet, once we have laughed with that, the fact remains: freedom from making demands on the other is a freedom from one's own habitual expectations, and any freedom from habit is first of all a lightening of oneself that is a gift. Enough lightening, and one approaches that source from which all such gifts are given. I call it godlike.

But all this access to the other is not just based in disinterest. An inevitable requirement of self is present: one must get what one needs from the other in order to give what the other needs. Now, this defining of basic need is not always easy, for various reasons. To a man I know who is consumed with self-doubt, for instance, believing in his own needs at all is difficult, so that he can hardly pay attention to whether or not they are being met. And the woman in his life is denied the pleasure of pleasing him. Another man is so bent on pleasing a woman, out of fear of losing her, that he fails to consult his needs, though he has begun to tell me quite specifically what they are: he wants a woman as a partner, he wants her as a soul-mate, he wants her to trust him. As to the man I described earlier: does he need to go on controlling his wife? Or could it be that, if *she* accepted him just as he is and dared to trust him with her money, he might then loosen the reins which she now resists and be for her more trustworthy? His own need for control follows from an earlier breakdown of trust, with parents who could not care for him freely, as he wished, and who gave affection only when he did what they wished. His wife meanwhile safeguards herself from him and, while loyal, can feel little of the love she wants to feel. It would be a crucial new freedom for them together, to discover that their controls aren't needed.

Much work in individual therapy centers on clarifying and supporting needs—for security with others, for creative expression, for selfless giving to others—and it is done through the therapist's seeing, from the patient's side, what the problems with needs have been. This seeing is called empathy. But it is by no means reserved for clinical situations. It prevails in successful intimate relationship; for to be given what one needs is to be empathically appreciated and validated by the other. Here is the second member of my list.

Mutual Empathy

Empathy, like trust, is possible because of the primal bond between people, which makes "seeing from the other side" possible. But though it arises from this bond, it depends on our own inherent sense of being variable: how different I could be from the way, by temperament and conditioning, I actually am; how different, therefore, yet comprehensible and valid to me, someone else actually is. Projections, which see the other person just from one's own side, may themselves foster empathy when they are positive. One is, for instance, passionately attached, devoted unto death, entirely at the disposal of the projected beloved whom one adores and exalts. But the empathy stays within the focal range of the projection, and often ends abruptly with its end. "What did I ever see in him, in her," we then say.

With empathy free from projection, what we see in him, in her persists. It grows in fact in significance, because the other, like oneself, changes, and new aspects develop to be noticed and responded to: the inward joy of a woman with her first baby, the loneliness of an old man who has just lost his wife of forty years. In psychotherapy, empathy itself is a chief fruit of the work. "It's very hard for my husband to take a criticism," a woman says with a fresh forbearance about him. So appreciated, he relaxes with her. "Under her tough front, I've just realized that she can be very soft," a man tells me about the woman in his life. And they both feel more connected. The more there is of empathy, the greater, too, is the curb on old projections which may still be evoked. A man commented to me about his wife: "She said, 'Don't drive so close to the car in front.' I thought, 'Just like my mother!' But I felt: I don't want to scare her and our safety really is at risk. I slowed down. We went on talking about something else."

Empathy, as one receives it, immediately honors one's own needs and limits. Then it's easier to say "No": to an action which I dislike, to closeness when I want to be left alone, to sex when it's the wrong time. I don't have to defend myself. He, or she, without attack or complaint, is likely to see what I mean. And then I'm freer too, between us, with the positive things I mean.

So a relationship gains in depth.

But what *are* the various things it's likely to mean? We reach my third item.

Psychic Polymorphism

"Polymorphism" may sound a distinctly pagan note among my categories of the sacred bond. We hear in the word the "polymorphous perverse" of childhood sexuality according to Freud, or the classical world's polymorphous gods who change into human mortals, swans, and bulls. I beg indulgence here in meaning something as variable as these, at times as playful, but really less capricious, something even with grace enough to be set in a church's stained glass window.

Lovers come first. Out of the depths of desire an image arises of the one who gives love its wings, and he, or she, looks for another in whom to feel that sense of flight. The image sustains Psyche when her jealous sisters push her off the cliff, and in the night, at her magic castle, when the lover she cannot see comes to her.[1] It sustains the searching knight as he challenges and slays dragons in his path.[2] All the first vows of love spring from it, and the traditional marriage vows hang from it as by a thread. For a much harder task follows. Psyche loses her dream, and then must use her mortal legs to pursue it again through many hardships. The knight must stay faithful to the winged image even when she is disguised as an ugly old witch.[3] All marriages struggle with the loss of the lover's face and must believe in and look for its re-discovery. The depth of the relationship depends on it; without it, the thread snaps. Partners who can confide in one another their unhappiness at what they have lost still do not have nearly enough; the needed intimacy occurs when two persons wish to share being happy and are happy in each other's happiness. Sexual fulfillment follows suit: from desire gratified, gratifying one's partner, and the partner's gratification in gratifying one's own desire.

These sharings speak of personal joys. But there is another psychic bond—companionship—which has a different form.

I mean: shared ventures, aspirations, and difficulties which extend beyond the partners themselves, in the nurture of a family, in concern for the world at large, in values as to a way of life and a view of life. From this widened sense, also each one can support the individuality of the other, through the vicissitudes of living in which hopes, plans, and forethought mingle with frustrations and unforeseeable chance events. Of course, love known through intimacy deepens the sense of comradeship, becomes the love, as Rilke says, in which "two solitudes protect and border and salute each other."[4] And without the comradeship, love itself would be confined, a special oasis, not a presence throughout one's world.

But all these equalities are just one side of the relationship. It thrives too on complementarities: wherein each partner at times is parent to the other when the need for that is felt. One of course gets lessons in being parental to one's spouse from being a real parent to one's children, but the capability is there without them. And the fact is that the spouse's occasional need of the partner is for an all-around parent, an *androgynous* parent, and for that, in fact, either the man or the woman will do. The need arises tumultuously. At one time the woman wants the man to stand beside her, as loving adult comrade, through a difficult career decision. At another time—it could be the next moment—the little girl in her wants him to be a maternal comfort, bringing a treat to her from the kitchen. At another, she wants a paternal support who will hear her dilemma and give lots of encouragement, without infantilizing her. On his part the man wishes the woman, as partner, to care about his successes and vexations. But when extreme loss or confusion bogs him down, the small boy in him wants her maternal protection from extra stress, and perhaps her paternal competence, too, taking over household affairs he usually manages while he regains his self-support.

The equal adult bonds, it's true, give the relationship its widest expression and deepest roots. The complementarities will sap it unless they are subordinate. When so provided, however, they grant the main roots rich branchings and nourishment.

But these ranges of need can only be asked for in a mate when the man and the woman each feel free to be so needful. With equal partners, this freedom in turn increases their own pleasure in responding to the other's need. Even when they both feel like needy children at the same time, usually one is a bit more able to rouse a parental strength, receptive solicitude or directive force or both, which in fact sets an example of self-nourishment for the other. Being "happy children together," of course, is in the repertoire of lovers. And if at times they must both lie in bed together like wounded dogs and groan, that too is a great comfort, and rather fun.

When pressed to explain, people in a good marriage sometimes say vaguely, "Well, I guess we share the right things." The "things," I would add, are all the varieties of psychic forms.

But so much matching of needs implies a steadfast sense of the relationship, as if, in the midst of one's varied wishes for independence, the shared life gratifies and continually rekindles a homing instinct. This does appear to be deep in us, and leads me to the last item on my list.

Mutual Commitment

"Commitment" is a double-edged word. It may mean a significant loss: the obvious loss, in marriage, of a single person's freedoms. It may mean a significant gain: the gain, in marriage, of an extended connection to the world. But inevitably this extension entails a dependence, and dependence sounds like a loss too, unless it is on someone who believes in one's right to privacy and need for occasions of independence. The interplay here with both trust and empathy is obvious—and also something else: for to receive this allowance from someone who cares for one, is to feel loved. To give it to someone one cares for, is to be loving. I think of Goethe's aphorism: "Voluntary dependence is the fairest state, and but for love, how would it be possible?"[5]

Commitment has the quality of a continuing project, one not taken for granted, kept fresh by constant tending to what it needs. This vigilance clearly applies to a garden one keeps, a book one writes, a child one rears. But in marriage it requires *mutuality* of the commitment. A friend of mine was married once to a very pretty, warm, flexible professional woman whom he cared for and who loved him. But she wanted to have children. He did not, and he did want to have affairs. She couldn't take it. They divorced. His second marriage, six years later, was to a more difficult woman, self-centered, prestige-minded, bickering. But this time, much more than before, he meant it. He loves her and is loyal; she appreciates him. They have two children in whom he delights.

Rejection of another's need undoes commitment. And on the receiving side, to feel rejected by someone one has trusted and come to love, whether clearheadedly or not, is to feel that dismaying gap, commitment's absence. The blunt truth, not usually so stated, for many of the women seduced by their male psychotherapists is not pain suffered from the inception of unprofessional behavior, but pain caused by the ending of it, or by the limits imposed on it. "He didn't really mean what he did. He didn't take the relationship into his heart." That is the outrage.

And yet constancy in relationship does not itself make for commitment, may even destroy it. A psychiatrist I know provides a special and sad example of this fact. His wife had grown jealous of a young woman in his practice whom she saw often, as his office was in their home and connected to it by a front hallway. She grew more upset after he had seen the patient in her own apartment a few times when she was ill. The woman did indeed care for him a great deal and at the time there was no other man in her life. But though he felt in good conscience about his work, with the continuing jealousy at home, cumulative, it seemed, over two years, he began to think of her as "the other woman" in his personal life, because of whom his wife was desperate and in tears. "It's strange," he told me much later. "I did that woman the same disservice *as if* I had seduced her. In a way, more so. Without her knowledge, I put her into my personal affairs. It never occurred to me then to consult with anyone about the problem, to move my office out of my home, to honor my commitment to *her*. One day, with no warning and refusing any explanation, I said our work must stop at once. She was startled, confused, wounded, and of course very angry. Six months later—my conscience kept biting me, I couldn't let the thing go—I found out through the man who had first referred her to me what happened to her. She had gotten herself *two* new therapists at the same time, in case one of them double-crossed her again. She was doing all right. But I wasn't. My action helped my marriage for a few months. My wife was grateful and I wasn't aware of my resentment. But what came over me, in time, was a feeling of removing myself. We had other problems, of course, but this one stayed with me as a crucial one. I wasn't with her any more." Now, twenty-five years later, long married to another woman and happy with her, he still recalls his action with remorse.

This event seems almost to predicate the failure of a marriage. And yet predictions are not possible. To elaborate what I have said before: the marriage doesn't exist which is without conflict, free of hurt, free of self-interest which causes the partner pain, or free (unless it's repressed) of a roving eye on others. At any age, passion can play strange tricks with the dedicated heart. And the most secure relationships may grow weedy with jabs, complaints, or the pained looks of "I won't say anything, but once again . . ." And yet, too, I believe that the attitude of an ideal commitment—call it an ideal fidelity—is quite possible, and nourishes a real fidelity that keeps the bloom fresh. In turn, however, people are only committed to this fidelity together when they are committed to an inner need for it, to the value of this concentration of themselves, and when they find the commitment, with no self-deception, quite right.

Once again we are referred back to the inner lives of each partner. Indeed trust, empathy, freedom of self-acceptance, and a need to commit oneself—all these factors of depth in relationship originate in the person's own depths; all these charities begin at home.

HARMONY OF THE INNER AND THE OUTER MARRIAGE

A relationship, then, can only be as deep, as sacred by the standards of this essay, as one's relationship to oneself. But a sense of the other may be a good measure of one's sense of self—perhaps most pointedly, one's sense of a stranger. What do I think of him, of her, as they just mind their own business, across the street, in an elevator, on the adjacent seat of the airplane? Do I assume good will? Threat? Potential demand? Nuisance? Judgment? Interesting complexity? A possible haven? These thoughts, of course, say something of my actual past experience with others, but most accurately they are an inner mirror: attitudes which I have toward myself and will, in consequence, finally find in another who becomes my intimate.

And for generous and confiding intimacy to develop, at the depth of the sacred, a further array of self-questioning confronts me. How much do I trust the scope of my moods? How accepting am I of the logic, and illogic, of needs, including those fears and inhibitions I want to be free of? How widely do I take myself in, as tender and adventuresome, wayward and obstinate, familiar and surprising, adult and child, male and female, source of powers known, latent, and unknown? How faithful am I to aspirations through trials and disappointments? How well do I discern *where* fidelity to myself really lies? Within marriage, it is often clear enough that infidelity to oneself is more a crime than infidelity to one's partner. And since we are more transparent than we like to think, most of the time this is what the aggrieved partner appraises in the aftermath of actual unfaithfulness. "He says it's really me he wants. But I don't believe him." Or, with hope, "I think I can believe him." Or, in a further inward question, "But do I any longer want *him*?"

As to the masculine and feminine within, I'm thinking of the contrast in expressiveness that Karen Blixen spoke about between *doing* and *being*: male action to achieve, female receptiveness to life as it is.[6] Made so wide, the distinction clearly includes the powers of each of us, our basic androgyny, and today it is understood to take variant forms in partnership. Not only with the parent-child complementarities as I have described them, but in homoerotic bonds which can have the depth and range of traditional marriage. The fitness of these bonds, again, rises from the depth of the partners' inner needs. However it's expressed, mutual love has one single requirement: that one be adored by the person one adores (not, alas, by another!). So, too, mutual commitment means that one receives devotion, as an essential blessing, from the person to whom one is devoted. All these fine things, in turn, emerge from a high self-esteem, so that in the first place the man and woman feel their own value to be undiminished by the high value of the intimate, and neither of them depends, for a sense of worth, on distancing or superior caste. Problems of self-esteem always defeat one's inner freedom, though they may take shrewdly practical forms. In many problematic but stable marriages, for instance, the feeling "I deserve better" competes with "No one is likely to put up with me any better, or even so well." And the latter wins out.

In a good marriage it is as though a mystery has been solved. But not in any rational form. One feels the solution as another mystery. Needs from the past, from one's depths, the needs that I have described for mutual trust, empathy, acceptance, and commitment, all are well met: one can say that precisely, but one cannot precisely say how; for what the partner does isn't quite the point. The point is that he, or she, *is the one*. And yet something of the partner's essence, too, remains ungraspable, a mystery different from one's own though resonant with it, like a flashing of signals between two enigmas. Only bad marriages are the ones one can explain. Their ill fit is visible and clear.

But the good marriage doesn't occur just by chance or by luck either, any more than migratory birds return to their breeding grounds by accident. A feeling of inner need is the guide, and one's acceptance of the need is already an *inner marriage* that leads to the outer one, whose rightness for the person comes from the sense that the two marriages are in harmony. There are vows for the inner marriage that become, in fact, the best prototype for the outer marriage; they must first of all be taken within oneself if they are to endure with a partner. I have formulated these in another place,[7] and repeat them here. "I take you, my inner life, my world, my fate, to be my lawful wedded kin" (so the words begin in traditional form. But then they change:) "to please and to trouble me, to understand and to misunderstand me, to let me be and to impose on me and to slight me, to be demanding and unreasonable, selfish and self-justified, unyielding and righteous and proud—I take you, in all, to honor and to cherish, as long as I shall live."

The inner vows are the initiatory rite for the outer marriage, and prepare one to make it holy.

In turn, the good outer marriage serves to fructify the inner one: the couple gives and receives all the more inwardly as each gives and receives in relationship. Through this interplay a long lasting marriage grows into a kind of organism of which the individuals are a part and who themselves reflect all of it in their separate living. Sometimes, in old age happily married people look like one another.

Given this perspective of the sacred, is there such a thing as "a good divorce"?

Yes, it follows directly: when the outer marriage, which depends on mutual vows and can't be brought off single-handed, does not correspond to the inner. Now, it's true that a singleminded ultimatum may bear fruit; we often change only when life serves up an "Or else." For instance, with a young couple I know, the man said to his wife in the first year of their marriage, "If you won't give up the daily fighting over trifles, let's not go on. I can't live like this. Don't worry. I'll be fair with you in settling money matters." The woman thought, "After all, I love him. This is ridiculous." She didn't say anything. But during the next weeks most of their quarreling stopped, and they decided together to buy a puppy dog.

Had she, instead, replied, "I don't take orders from anyone!" and stuck with it, the flag would have come down on empathy and commitment, and the marriage would probably be over.

On the other hand, many bad marriages persist, as I've said, from fear of something worse, or they defy spontaneity for the sake of family, career, or other expedients. Nor is all actual divorce well considered by both partners, no more than all marriages begin with inner marriages. But at best it provides an important schooling in what one needs that one did not get, and what the partner needs that one could not give. Psychologically, the marriage hasn't been consummated; the two do better with one another, if at all, from a distance; and divorce amounts to what the Catholic Church calls an annulment.

Such developments are painful, the end of a dream, the grief of a loss, reminders that living, in its sum of difficulties and strengths, is inevitably insecure. Certainly our days pass in unceasing change, and quickly. "Life flies by like a dance," a song of Mozart sings.[8] The great Chinese poet of the 8th century, Tu Fu, has a grimmer image: "Life whirls past like drunken wildfire."[9] Can a relationship, by the absoluteness of its commitment, redeem this whirligig? Find in the pledges of its partners a depth to which there is no wear and tear? One feels, to look at her face, that Mother Teresa made that kind of marriage. So may we all, from the knowledge of our needs and the devotion of our hearts.

NOTES

1. The tale, "Cupid and Psyche," is told in Chapters 7–9 of Apuleius, *The Golden Ass*.

2. The Arthurian romances treat this theme seriously: for instance, Malory's *Morte d'Arthur*. Cervantes' *Don Quixote* treats it comically, but with tenderness.

3. See "The Wife of Bath's Tale" in Chaucer's *The Canterbury Tales*. It's easiest to read in Theodore Morrison's translation from the Middle English, although the wings of the original are clipped.

4. From the seventh letter of Rilke's *Letters to a Young Poet*.

5. From Goethe's "Maxims and Reflections," Number 1120 of these in the published German listing (see *Goethes Werke*, Band XII, C. H. Beck,

Munchen, 1973). In English, it is given a whole page to itself (p. 143) in the collection, *Goethe's World View*.

6. From her address, "Oration at a Bonfire, Fourteen Years Later," published under the pseudonym Isak Dinesen in *Daguerreotypes and Other Essays*.

7. "Psychotherapy as Sacred Ground," *Journal of Humanistic Psychology*, Winter, 1991.

8. The poem, "Evening Thoughts" (in German, "Abendempfindung") is by Joachim Heinrich Campe. The text is only available in the United States as the German words to Mozart's song. Lieder recitals sometimes provide translations.

9. From the third poem in *One Hundred Poems from the Chinese*, Kenneth Rexroth, translator. With so much reworked in this translation, he is credited on the title page as the author of the book.

REFERENCES

Apuleius (1951). *The Golden Ass*. Robert Graves, translator. New York: Farrar, Straus, & Giroux.

Cervantes Saavedra, Miguel de (1960). *Don Quixote*. Samuel Putnam, translator. New York: The Viking Press.

Campe, Joachim Heinrich (undated). Abendempfindung. *Mozart Lieder*. New York: C. F. Peters.

Chaucer, Geoffrey (1977). *The Portable Chaucer*. Theodore Morrison, translator. New York: Penguin Books.

Dinesen, Isak (1979). *Daguerreotypes and Other Essays*. Chicago: The University of Chicago Press.

Goethe, Johann Wolfgang von (1963). *Goethe's World View*. Heinz Norden, translator. New York: Frederick Ungar Publishing Co.

Malory, Sir Thomas (1986). *Morte d'Arthur*. New York: Penguin Books.

Rexroth, Kenneth (1965). *One Hundred Poems from the Chinese*. New York: New Directions Books.

Rilke, Rainer Maria (1954). *Letters to a Young Poet*. M. D. Herter Norton, translator. New York: W. W. Norton & Company, Inc.

Schoen, Stephen (1991). "Psychotherapy as Sacred Ground." *Journal of Humanistic Psychology*, 31(1), 51–55.

The Spirit of Home

Kris Jeter

And when they say, "You-all come back"—they don't mean it!

Burt Reynolds, *Evening Shade*

Love can build a bridge
    between your heart and mind.
Love can build a bridge
    Don't you think it's time?
    Don't you think it's time?

Naomi and Wynnona Judd, *Love Can Build a Bridge.*

Lee and Floyd met on a train from points west to Manhattan Island. Lieselotte, the daughter of German immigrants, was a voice student of soprano Dorothee Manski of the Metropolitan Opera in New York City and music major at Western Reserve University in Cleveland, Ohio. Floyd Olan, son of an East Texas rural family, was a Chief Petty Officer

Kris Jeter, PhD is Principal, Beacon Associates, Ltd., Inc., Newark, DE. She is the Director of Programs and Communications for The Possible Society. Dr. Jeter is the Analytic Essay Editor for the international journal, *Marriage & Family Review.* She is the author of over 50 publications and the producer of over 50 photo essays and illustrated lectures. Her scholarly work is on the family over the life cycle; utilizing the family as a unit of analysis in research; and examining its important linkages and interactions with larger bureaucratic organizations. Dr. Jeter incorporates in her work international anthropology, archaeology, art, history, literature, mythology, religion, sociology, and psychology. She is interested in the programming, facilitation, and evaluation of the affective, cognitive, and psychomotor learning processes using various techniques.

115

in the U.S. Navy. For three years they corresponded. They devised a code so that despite censorship, Lee would know exactly where Floyd was stationed. Toll house cookies provided a taste of home while he was in Great Britain. Autumn leaves reminded Floyd of America while he was in the South Pacific. With each exchange, love deepened.

When Floyd was stationed stateside in Boston, despite their plans for a long engagement, love overruled and they married. Upon his military discharge, they put their belongings in an automobile and drove to his native state and homeland, Texas.

All was well until they pulled into an Arkansas gasoline station for fuel. To Lee, the attendant spoke what seemed a foreign language. More important, though, was that Floyd responded—speaking this same corruption of the English language. In three years of correspondence interspersed with military leaves in Cleveland, Lee had never heard Floyd talk as a "good ole country boy"! She was dazed. The crowning affront occurred as they were starting to drive away. The gasoline attendant yelled, "You-all come back now, you hear!" Silently, trying to interpret this new language, she asked herself, why would a proprietor command people to go out of their way to spend money at his business? She sat in the car crying, wondering who this stranger was that she had married. Romance was punctured by the reality of differences. What was the chance of their dissimilar spirits surviving, much less thriving in such an unlikely marriage? Could love build a bridge between two hearts and minds? Would Lee and Floyd ever feel at home again with each other?

Lee and Floyd are my parents. They celebrated 37 anniversaries, their marriage ending with the death of Lee in 1981. Lee related the Arkansas revealing story to me as an adult, laughing about this chapter in their marriage. Yet, this account was only the first of many chronicles about two free spirits striving to co-exist and nurture each other, me, and many.

What caused Lee and Floyd to meet? What attracted Lee and Floyd to each other? Capricious fortuity plays a primary role in human love, as in life. The union of two people is predicated on love, an indescribable whimsical yet innate feeling. Likewise, vagarious chance predestines a person's expression of spirituality, an ineffable, incalculable, yet intrinsic human experience. Love and spirituality activate persons to grow, alone or together. In this analytic essay, I explore the expression of spirituality by couples and families. Couplehood challenges each partner's embodiment and manifestation of spiritual passion.

SPIRITUALITY: JOURNEY TO HOME

You will go to new places—
Your eyes will always go backward . . . toward home.

—Cochese, Apache Chief
Broken Arrow

The word spirituality is derived from the Latin word, *spirare*, to breathe. Spirituality is the breath of life, vital power, animating energy within human beings, interacting between heart and mind, body and soul.

Life in a womb is remembered as warm, secure; all needs are satisfied. Exile, though, is our inborn, native condition. The shock of birth shoves the newborn from a serene, silent, stable haven to an agitated, aggressive, apprehensive universe. The womb is the ultimate, the sentimental home. Upon being thrust into the world, life becomes a struggle where each need is met or not met by a pair of female and male parents and guardians. The primary home is lost and the balance of life is spent remembering and yearning for its splendor. Ensuing effort is directed toward attempting to return to the home—emotional, mental, physical, and spiritual home.

The physical act of homecoming is most often connected with religious holidays, spiritual holy days. Jewish families gather together for Passover, the celebration of the exodus from slavery in Egypt, and for the High Holy Days, the remembrance of God's benevolence, justice, and supremacy. Muslim families assemble to end the month of day time fasting, Ramadan, with the celebration of the Feast of Fast Breaking. The devout pray for the illumination of the world that accompanied the revelation of the Koran.

In the United States during the last two weeks of December 1990, 34.8 million Americans disregarded an economic shift and increased gasoline expenses to travel by airplane, automobile, or train to be with kin ("From Atlantic to Pacific"). The longing of Christians and others to gather at Christmas is a profound fundamental passion. This intense emotion compels action. The behavior may even be paralleled to migration patterns. Selected animals, birds, and fish return each winter to their birthplace to bear offspring who will continue the species. Likewise, people return to their family home during the period of solstice, the shortest days of sunlight in the northern hemisphere, to celebrate the birth of a Messiah who will save the world. People surrender to the call, disregarding financial costs and other obligations, simply to return home.

People go home for Christmas, even though they may come down with the newly identified syndrome, Holiday Blues. Holiday Blues is caused, in part, by unrealistic expectations. The physical act of homecoming is expected to satisfy deep-seated emotional, mental, and spiritual longings for home. Rather, financial pressures accelerate. There doesn't seem to be enough energy or time to complete every obligation. Many persons gather together who, at the most, talk to or write each other once a year. Embarrassed at their lack of communication and filled with liquid cheer, they may drift into argument. Gifts which may seem special to the presenter may not be truly appreciated by a receiver who is immersed in the materialistic culture. Children of divorced parents may feel like pawns. They have multiple functions to attend, gifts to give, and loyalties to maintain. Domestic violence increases.

To cure and prevent Holiday Blues, therapists recommend that boundaries be established. Many nuclear families decide that Christmas Day is to be enjoyed within their home. Other holidays, such as St. Nicholas Day, Christmas Eve, the Feast Day of the Holy Innocents, New Year's Eve, New Year's Day, and the Twelfth Night, are celebrated with the wider family. Extended families may choose to hold annual lotteries to concentrate shopping efforts of each person to just one gift. Cultivating an intimate knowledge of the prospective recipient transforms the work of shopping into pleasurable pursuit. A gift for the "person who has everything" may be a donation to charity made in her or his name. Families may spend Christmas working at a soup kitchen, returning home thankful for the blessings bestowed upon them.

Christmas is the time when we traditionally give tokens of love. Christmas can be the time we give love—the pure essence of the heart. The love of the deity expressed through humans is creative, redemptive goodwill. Hate can be seen as a burden too great to bear. The song, "I'll be home for Christmas," is sung with renewed understanding. The saying, "Home is where the heart is," is repeated with deeper comprehension.

The word home is derived from the Old Norse word, *heimr*, which means abode or world (Neilson). The allure of home tugs us from unsettled wayfaring to find our promised land, wellspring, veritable self. Home, protected and intimate is remote, yet consummate within our very breath. Spirituality is the voyage from our common fundamental estrangement to our universal, essential world.

In 1989, I asked the Venerable Khenpo Palden Sherab Rinpoche and the Venerable Khenpo Tsewang Dongyal Rinpoche, Nyingma lamas (in exile from Tibet since 1960) what were the lessons they had learned as refugees. They responded that upon going into exile, they took with them a roadmap, the teachings of the Vajrayana tradition to use as their guide. This guide teaches and reminds them to live with love and compassion. The exile has forced them to live with love and compassion. The exile has forced them to leave their retreat in Tibet to live and teach their ways around the globe. They have learned that their home is within their hearts and that they are truly at their own abode in lower Manhattan or wherever they reside on this world. The diaspora, the scattering, the sowing of seeds across the earth, nourishes the spiritual home within the cosmos.

INTEGRATED THEORY OF SPIRITUALITY

Spirit that breathest through my lattice: . . . I welcome
    thee
To the scorched land, thou wanderer of the seal. . . .
Go,—but the circle of eternal change,
    Which is the life of nature, shall restore,
With sounds and scents from all thy mighty range,
    Thee to thy birthplace of the deep once more.

—William Cullen Bryant, *The Evening Wind.*

For the past thirty years professionals in business, development, education, medicine, and social services have applied Abraham Maslow's hierarchy of needs to their work with individuals. I, myself, taught nurses in the early 1970's how to evaluate the status of a client by using Maslow's hierarchy. To review Maslow's Theory, individuals must satisfy a level of needs before they can satisfy the next level.

There are five levels of need. The first level includes the basic needs of food, water, and reproductive sex. The second need is shelter. The third need is love and a sense of belongingness. The fourth is self-esteem. The highest need is self-actualization, realization of unity with all life. Maslow believed that individuals satisfy waves of needs, for instance focusing on two levels at the same time. In the past several years, it has been the vogue for individuals to speak of themselves as self-actualized. Actually, Maslow felt that only a few individuals ever achieved self-actualization, such persons as Mohandas Gandhi, Albert Schweitzer, Mother Theresa, and Harriet Tubman.

Acknowledging Maslow for his very positive contribution to the humanization of our world, I would like to propose an addition to his thinking. I propose that we transform the one hierarchical pyramid into two interlocked pyramids, a symbol that mythologists call King Solomon's Seal and the Star of David. The survival of the world depends upon the incorporation of the spirit of unity, the concept of self-actualization within every act of life (Jeter, 1989). The acts of obtaining food, water, reproductive sex plus shelter need to be interposed with the spirit of thankfulness, celebration, and unity "within the circle of eternal change."

ARCHETYPES OF SPIRITUALITY AND THE FAMILY

The stories of the Hebrew Bible, Christian Bible, Koran, and religious commentaries are rich, providing varied characters, role models, and prototype options for living. Immersed in the depths of the human psyche is the universal, primordial, collective unconscious inhabited by archetypes, internal forces of energy which seek to organize the psyche's varied interactions and sustain the endurance of the ego consciousness. These archetypes are spontaneously expressed cross culturally as vital life forces and archetypal images in art, fantasies, dreams, fairy tales, and myths. It is through the archetypal images that the human being reveals profound unconscious longings and yearnings (Jung).

Judaism, Christianity, and Islam utilize Genesis to trace a common ancestry to the patriarch Abraham and his wider family. The exalted father Abraham is considered to be the first human in Chaldea to know and praise God. Yielding to God's call, seventy-five-year-old Abram and sixty-five-year-old Sarai led their large entourage of workers and herds over the fertile crescent to settle in an unheard-of territory. Here a covenant is cut; God tells Abram that despite his advanced age, he will have a son and that his name is now Abraham, "father of many nations." Sarai's name is changed to Sarah; both of her names mean "princess."

Sarah does indeed bear a child, Isaac. At God's command, steadfast and trustworthy Abraham prepares to sacrifice Isaac on an altar. As the knife is to be inserted, a ram is revealed to be utilized instead. God reiterates the pledge that Abraham's descendants will increase "as the stars of heaven."

Archetypes abound in this story that still incise and ignite humankind today: "the covenant," "the chosen people," "the promised land." Abraham is the archetype of impeccable and enduring belief, the loyal "friend of God." His is a life of conviction and surrender despite adversity. Abraham is also, according to Susan Niditch, the archetype of the trickster who as a minority underdog, displays cunning and adaptability to triumph in the larger culture. Because of the graciousness he expressed to three strangers, Abraham is the patron saint of hospitality (Jeter, 1991).

Over the years, when reading Genesis plus related books and visiting archaeological sites, I, like others, have noted inconsistencies. Commentators in the main have either accepted without question or ignored these incongruities. Some have created elaborate explanations. In the spirit of the classical oral tradition, the story has been expanded, it is hoped by each story teller, for the better. However, it is these very additions that fabricate an intricate mystery for later historians to investigate. Savina J. Teubal has conducted careful, extensive historical cross-cultural research on ancient Middle Eastern art and texts. What emerges is a portrayal of a culture in transition. The patriarchal story is evident; yet, buried as if in the lower part of an iceberg lies the less evident, deeper matriarchal story. Indeed, Teubal has identified five characteristics of the matriarchal social environment in Genesis.

1. Rigorous ordinances prescribe family membership. Primary families consist of uterine siblings.
2. Because ancestry is determined by matrilineal descent, endogamy or marriage of a woman to a brother by her father can occur.
3. A pattern in Genesis and in matrilineal descent is ultimogeniture; the youngest receives the legacy.
4. In a matrilocal society, the man when married relocates

from his home to live with his wife in an extended family of kindred women and their imported spouses.
5. Sororal polygyny occurs in matrilocal families with a limited number of progeny. To compensate for small family size, two or more sisters marry one man. Thus, he is charged by a number of marriage contracts to support this kinship network plus future children.

Teubal, in her translation from original sources of the story of Abraham, has identified four adult women. Sarah, Hagar, and Keturah are well known. The fourth woman is called by Teubal the Desert Matriarch.

Sarah

The Pharaoh of Egypt and later the King of Gerar recognize Sarai to be an esteemed priestess. They engage her to officiate as the goddess incarnate in the ritual of the hieros gamos, the sacred marriage to insure the fertility of the land. In the tradition of ancient Mesopotamian priestesses, Sarai chooses to be childless and selects the sexual partners of her husband.

Abram is associated with commerce and trade hubs: Bethel, Damascus, Haran, Hebron, Shechem, and Ur. These sites are also sacred sites, groves for the consultation of oracles and temples for the worship of the moon. In Shechem, the "Navel of the Land," under the terebinth tree of Moreh, an oracle reveals that land would be provided to Abram, Sarai, and their children. Sarai resides most of her life in Mamre, a grove of sacred terebinth trees. She lives in a tent woven of reeds associated with the storehouse of the Middle Eastern goddess.

Abraham purchases the Cave of Machpelah near Mamre for the grave of Sarah. Machpelah becomes the burial site for the sons chosen by the matriarch. Likewise, Hebrew progenitors are selected by the matriarchs to be in their lineage. Even today, Jewish identity can be determined by endogamy symbolized by the circumcision of males and, also, matriliny, being a child of a Jewish mother.

Sarah represents the primal matriarchal culture and Abraham the later patriarchal schema. Royalty fear Sarah as a relative of the goddess; they rebuke Abram. Sarah is a priestess who ritually embodies the goddess. Abraham acts as an intercessor between God and his people and does God's bidding without question.

Hagar

Hagar is the shifhah, companion of Sarah, who probably joined Sarah when she was in Egypt. "Hagar is the only woman in the Bible who, protected by her personal god, receives the promise that she (via her son) will become a great nation" (Teubal, 1990, page 168).

The spiritual journeys of Sarah and Hagar have similar facets. Sarah from Ur and Hagar from Egypt are removed from their homelands and families by birth to live in Hebron as expatriates in Canaan and within the wider family of Abraham. They probably live as virgin priestesses. In later life, a male child is born to Hagar and then to Sarah. Each is selected by her deity to be the matriarch of a community.

The Desert Matriarch

Savina J. Teubal in her careful research has identified a third woman, the Desert Matriarch. Genesis 16:7–15 and Genesis 21:14–21 tell the story of a woman who is lost in the desert with a small boy in need of water to survive and the divine showing of a well. This child is named Ishmael and becomes an archer. Teubal proposes that the derivation of the story of the Desert Matriarch may be the story of Neith. Neith, portrayed with arrows is the pre-dynasty Egyptian Goddess of the War and the Hunt. Geography and the age of the son point to two stories that have commonly been interpreted as one story about Hagar.

Hagar wandered in the desert outside of Beersheva that is near two trade routes, the Way of the Red Sea between Sodom and Elat and the Way of Mt. Seir between Elat and

Memphis. Rocks protrude out of the sand to define the territory. The Desert Matriarch wandered and got lost in the Desert of Shur, a stretch of indistinguishable sand dunes in the northern Sinai.

Hagar's son is a ha-na'ar or lad of marriageable age. The Desert Matriarch's son is a ha-yeled or a small child who is carried upon the mother's shoulder.

The Desert Matriarch designates herself, "raiti ahrei ro'i, I who saw [deity] after my vision." The Desert Matriarch is the only human in the Hebrew Bible to formulate a name for the deity who redeems her and her infant son. She calls the deity "El-ro'i, the visionary or seeing god" (Teubal, 1990, page 196). Her son's life, not Hagar's, is rescued with water from a well. In return, the young boy is called Ishmael or the god heard the Desert Matriarch pleading for water.

Sarah, Hagar, and the Desert Matriarch display aspects of the spiritual leader. Sarah "hears" and "listens." Abraham is told by the deity, "Whatever Sarah tells you listen to her voice" (Genesis 21:12). Sarah may have been a priestess who, like the oracles of Delphi, prophesied and spoke revelation. Hagar and the Desert Matriarch "look" and "see." They may have been dreamers, visionaries, utopians.

Keturah

As a trader, Abraham had extended his territory toward the south known for its fragrant balms. After Sarah dies, Abraham marries Keturah whose name means incense. She is the matriarch of six Arabian communities including the Medan, Midian, Joskhan, and Zimran tribes (Teubal, 1984, Page 95).

There is very limited information about Keturah and her geographic home and spiritual beliefs. We do know about the widespread and ever increasing use and value of incense. Possibly, Abraham after having been associated with priestesses was consciously looking for a career woman. Perhaps, Keturah and Abraham are archetypes of the dual career traders!

CONCLUSION

Sometimes I feel like a motherless child. Sometimes I
feel like a motherless child. Sometimes I feel like a
motherless child,   A long way from home.

—Black American Spiritual

We live in an era of rapid change, so speedy and uncertain
that, at times, we feel all like a motherless child. Archetypes
revered for millennia in art and mythology are now exploited
by advertising companies. These muddled images, mixed
concepts confront, affront us over the airwaves and in print.
Moreover, they confound us as we conduct our daily life.
Curators of the exhibit, "High and Low: Modern Art and
Popular Culture" for the Museum of Modern Art collected
advertising, caricature, comics, and graffiti developed from
1890 to 1968 and compared this work to modern art. They
conclude: "The interworkings of society and art in our era
seem to bear out a surprising aphorism: nothing so sacred
that it may not be profaned, but nothing so profane that it
may not be made, in a sense sacred" ("A Wheel, Not a
Ladder").

For instance, to many, the Madonna is no longer the virgin
of miraculous birth in a long dress of red, covered with a blue
cape, who becomes the earth mother cradling the savior
child. She is not immediately recalled as the madonna of
adoration enthroned in majesty, protector of passages, pro-
vider of mercy, queen of heaven.

To followers of the American popular culture, Madonna is
a woman who wears black lace underwear as outerwear and
holds her crotch in public. She is the star of several anti-
establishment music video's. "Papa Don't Preach" provides
a role model for uneducated, uninformed adolescent pregnancy. "Express Yourself" portrays the sexual option of
being bound in chains. ABC's *Nightline* aired Madonna's
December 1990 video banned by MTV, Cable's Music Televi-
sion. "Justify My Love" depicts explicit sexual fantasies

complete with leather harnesses and Nazi caps. The video, played in the entirety, was followed by an interview with Madonna. *Nightline* enjoyed the second highest ratings in its ten-year history. This Madonna is an archetype of belligerence, dynamism, entrepreneurship, materialism, pretension, pugnacity, and sexuality.

Today, lives are longer and more complex than ever before in history. Albert Einstein entwined space and time into one unique, incessantly teasing enigma. To survive and thrive in such actual and perceptual chaos, couples and families are in need of profound archetypes and unifying spirituality. The popular culture Madonna presents only flimsy lightweight underwear in which to meet the world. The floor length, coarse fabric cloak of the ancient Madonna provides time-honored love and protection.

Abraham and the Matriarchs are archetypes for families living between eras. The Matriarchs retain their unique spiritual beliefs while with Abraham, the proponent for monotheism. Gender equity is slowly reemerging into human history.

Archaeological remains indicate that marriage contracts were common in the ancient Middle East and probably transacted between Abraham and Sarah. Varied cultural groups including Jews have over the ages negotiated and written marriage contracts. Today, cohabitation and marriage contracts are favored by larger numbers of Westerners. The couple takes the opportunity to discuss their past, present, and future while formalizing their commitment (Sussman and Jeter).

Abraham and the Matriarchs are the archetypes for the bi-coastal, commuter, dual career, and dual home marriage. Abraham and Keturah as career traders traveled extensively. Sarah preferred to live in Mamre, a grove of sacred terebinth trees. Hagar became the matriarch of Mecca, the sacred city of Islam. The Desert Matriarch had powers associated with the Egyptian Goddess Neith. Sarah, Hagar, and the Desert Matriarch had the powers of priestesses and were known for their dreams, oracles, and visions.

Most important, Sarah and Abraham are a prominent ar-

chetype of the couple; they illustrate the primacy of couplehood. Today, after four thousand years of oral tradition and
over two thousand years of written tradition, the foundation
couple of Christianity and Judaism is Sarah and Abraham.
Even though Abraham is associated with Hagar, the shifhah;
the Desert Matriarch; and upon the death of Sarah, a second
wife, Sarah is considered Abraham's principal partner. The
traditional burial site for Sarah and Abraham, as well as Eve
and Adam, Leah and Jacob, plus Rebecca and Isaac is the
Cave of Machpelah in Hebron. Machpelah, located in what is
today called the West Bank of the Jordan River, is considered
sacred to Christians, Jews, and Muslims and contains the
remains of a Byzantine church and an active synagogue and a
functioning mosque.

American family life with all of its options, is difficult for
Westerners and Easterners to understand. The Iraqies in
December 1990 had a counterpart to the World War II Japa-
nese radio announcer, Tokyo Rose (Ellis). Baghdad Betty
informed the American military men serving in Saudia Arabia
that while they were away, their wives were dating Bart
Simpson—a cartoon character with bulging eyes and hair
combed high, standing straight up, cut in zig zags!

Inter-marriage is common place in the United States—
inter-marriage between persons of different careers, chrono-
logical ages, ethnicities, political creeds, religions, and socio-
economic background. Spiritual integrity seems difficult today. Selections of options and integration of innumerable
roles is a burden.

Yet, *hiero gamos* represents the ultimate harmony, the
conjugality of opposite characteristics in which the differences are surpassed; however each individual continues to be
a distinct person. This concept may be related to anthropolo-
gist Edward Sapir's theory of Hybrid Vigor. He observed that
in intermarriage, the best genetically coded traits are passed
on to their offspring. With sufficient time and intermarriage,
the similarities of each person's search for the spiritual home
could be acknowledged, differences respected. Spirituality,
the breath of life, vital power, animating energy could mediate

between the heart and mind, body and soul of the individual, couple, family, and community. The survival of the world depends upon the incorporation of the spirit of unity, and the concept of self-actualization within every act of life "within the circle of eternal change."

REFERENCES

Ellis, D. (21 January 1991). Have a Cow, G.I.! *Time*, 137(3)19.
Hill, D. B. (1957). *Abraham: His Heritage and Ours*. Boston, MA: Beacon Press.
The Holy Bible (—). The King James Version. Cleveland, OH: The World Publishing Company.
Jacoby, M. (1985). *The Longing for Paradise: Psychological Perspectives on an Archetype*. M. B. Gubitz, Translator. Boston, MA: Sigo Press.
Jeter, K. (1991). Hospitality: An Ancient Proponent for the Wider Family. *Marriage and Family Review: The Wider Family*, 17(1/2).
Jeter, K. (1989). Partnership Cultures. *Marriage and Family Review: Cross-Cultural Perspectives on Families, Work, and Change*, 14(1/2).
Jung, C. G. (1969). *The Archetypes and the Collective Unconscious*. Second Edition. Translated by R. F. C. Hull. Princeton, NJ: Princeton University Press.
The Museum of Modern Art (7 October 1990–15 January 1991). A Wheel, Not a Ladder. *High and Low: Modern Art and Popular Culture*. New York, NY: The Museum of Modern Art. 1.
Neilson, W. A. (Ed.) (1955). *Webster's New International Dictionary of the English Language*. Second Edition. Unabridged. Springfield, MA: Merriam Company, Publishers, 1191.
Niditch, S. (1987). *Underdogs and Tricksters: A Prelude to Biblical Folklore*. San Francisco, CA: Harper and Row, Publishers.
Patai, Raphael (1986). *The Seed of Abraham*. Salt Lake City, UT: University of Utah Press.
Peters, F. E. (1982). *Children of Abraham*. Princeton, NJ: Princeton University Press.
The Philadelphia Inquirer, (21 December 1990). *From Atlantic to Pacific*, D1.
Rinpoche, K. P. S. and K. T. D. Rinpoche (August 1989). *Buddhist Psychology*. Wilmington, DE: Padmasambhava Meditation Center.
Sapir, P. (Ed.) (1989). *The Collected Works of Edward Sapir*. New York, NY: DeGruyter.
Sussman, M. B. and K. Jeter (1985). Each Couple Should Develop a Marriage Contract Suitable to Themselves. *Current Controversies in Marriage and Family*. Beverly Hills, California: Sage Publications.

Teubal, S. J. (1990). *Hagar the Egyptian: The Lost Tradition of the Matriarchs.* San Francisco, CA: Harper and Row, Publishers.

Teubal, S. J. (1984). *Sarah the Priestess: The First Matriarch of Genesis.* Athens, OH: Swallow Press.

Van Seters, J. (1975). *Abraham in History and Tradition.* New Haven, CT: Yale University Press.

Woolley, Leonard (1936). *Abraham.* London, England: Faber and Faber Limited.

POEM

Judith Morley

Oh my dear
I can just see your heart
wondering
what long awaited gift
to buy me
for my birthday.

Don't try so hard
my beloved.

Just stand
in the kitchen
when I come down
for breakfast
and hold me
without drifting away.

Give me time
To breathe in
the fragrance
of you.

Don't think of the coffee
Bubbling out of the pot

or of the train
puffing to the station

131

or of the newspaper
waiting to be read

or of the clients
eager to be seen

Don't think even
of beguiling bedrooms
or of sex

Just stand in the kitchen
and hold me

That is all the gift I need
and it doesn't

come
in a
box!

For Product Safety Concerns and Information please contact our EU representative GPSR@taylorandfrancis.com Taylor & Francis Verlag GmbH, Kaufingerstraße 24, 80331 München, Germany

Batch number: 08153776

Printed by Printforce, the Netherlands